Moving on and Sta

Kirk Smith

Kirk Nathaniel Publishers

New York London San Salvador Bucharest Singapore Dallas Guayaquil

Introduction

Dear future, meek reader who inherited the earth. If you are in the year 2120 and wondering what life was like back in good ole 2020, I'll tell you. It was complicated.

Enclosed you'll find a brief summary of some of that year's events in no particular order. There were murder hornets. Australia had its most devastating wildfires the like of which had not been seen in over 100 years. Kobe, a famous basketball player, died along with nine other people in a chopper crash. George Floyd was killed, resulting in protests in over a hundred countries about the treatment of black people. There were earthquakes everywhere. Oh yeah, devastating locust swarms in Africa and Pakistan. The #MeToo Movement celebrated a powerful man being rightfully sent to prison. The impeachment and acquittal of a sitting US president. The UK withdrew from the EU. The US withdrew from the World Health Organization. Oh, and there is a global pandemic that up till now has killed hundreds of thousands of people and as I am writing this July 1, there are still six months to go. I mean at this point, even an asteroid is possible. A few years ago, the Mayan calendar was all over the news. Researchers and scientists said the Mayans predicted the end of the world in December 2012. Maybe the Mayans were off by eight years and the end of the world is December 2020, not 2012.

I have a friend Dustin, who is a comedian and actor. He was sure the world was going to end December 2012. In December 2011 he bought a whole living room set on credit.

Salesman, "Ok, it is interest free, but you have to start to pay in December 2012."

Dustin in his typical mix of Texas and SoCal accent, "We are all going to have to pay in 2012 man."

Living room furniture may seem like an odd thing to buy if the world is going to end, but that is where he spent most of his time. Why not go out in a blaze of glory, on a brand new sectional and coffee table. The world did not end, and Dustin paid for his couch out of his residuals from the movie Hop.

While Dustin is a little disorganized, in general he is right. It's all going to work out, until it doesn't. No need to fret. It's all good.

These are a series of short stories about my crazy little life during a crazy time. I hope they inspire you. Be encouraged, anything is possible. You got this, it's just life.

Movin Road Map

Stuck in the Middle

Everything has changed, day-to-day life this year has been a little weird. Here was this week's Monday.

My alarm clock goes off at 7:00 a.m. Today is a moving day, again. Not for me, but for some couple I was hired to move from Park Slope in Brooklyn to Princeton, NJ. Standup comedy is mostly at night, so I became a mover during the day. Not out of my undying love of carrying peoples' heavy garbage around, and believe me it's mostly garbage, but because it seemed like it would be easy and fast way to earn money. "I'm big, how hard can it be?" It's simple, yes, but not easy. What's the difference? For example, running a marathon is simple but not easy. It's simple, just run, but after blisters form on your feet, and ungodly chaffing and cramps have you praying, you realize this is not easy.

This is my first week working and I am on probation. Basically, if I drop anything or crash the truck I am fired. Normally being fired from a dead end job wouldn't be a cause for concern but these are not normal times, most of the city is shut down and I need the money.

I have two kids, Alex and JJ. JJ is the youngest and is disabled. He is 22 now with a man's body and a child's mind. His official diagnosis is autism and cognitively delayed, with a pinch of epilepsy and a few other little things added in for good measure. If I had to put a number on his age, I would say he's about five in his mind; there is an innocence that should have long since departed, but lingers on. He lives in Sweden (more about that later) in a home with other disabled people. They need a car for errands, doctor trips and joy rides. I'm living in New York City, but with the city mostly closed there is not much work. So, I decided to take a moving job to cover some expenses and to also buy him a car.

Every week more and more couples move out of the city from a cramped one-bedroom place to an actual little bungalow or a two-story house somewhere 50 miles from the city. Will they be happy? Who knows? But the city holds little appeal when everything is closed, and people are trying to social distance, which is nearly impossible in the city. I get the departures. Today it's Rachel and Sam's turn.

Starting in Greenpoint, I make my way down to Park Slope. Taking the A train to the F train with a 10-minute walk on each end, it takes me an hour to get there. The subway is mostly empty. There are a handful of frightened passengers on the train. No talking, little eye contact. We are approaching what feels like the end of the beginning of the pandemic, but only time will tell. There are fewer musicians in the subway these days. I see none today. I do see an older man asking for change. I tell him I don't have any, which in this case is true. I rarely have change these days. But for good measure I reach into my pocket to see if I have cigarettes, but I strike out on that count too. I don't smoke. It holds literally zero appeal to me.

My kids' late mom used to smoke, and I used to buy her cigarettes from the duty-free shop when I was traveling, as it was cheaper. Out of force of habit, I bought her cigarettes for several years after she passed away. It's funny the things you do without thinking. Like a Pavlovian dog, trained to do things they are not even interested in. Maybe this is how a dog feels when they fetch the paper. I remember turning around one day and realizing I had many cartons of cigarettes in my pantry. One time, I had a homeless person that I would see almost every day on the way to a comedy club ask me for a cigarette instead of money. I remembered the cartons of cigarettes at home. The next day, I gave him a pack. He was ecstatic, a pack of cigarettes can cost more than drugs in NYC. That's when a straight, middle-aged guy who looks like a Bible salesman started handing out cancer sticks. I could not decide if it was a kind or an evil deed. I had asked a local pastor who worked with the homeless down in the Bowery Mission if he thought that was a sin.

"What do you mean, is it a sin?" he replied.

"Well, I mean cigarettes cause cancer," I said.

"Oh, yeah, I mean they do, but that is the least of their problems. Cigarettes are a step in the right direction compared to drugs or booze. No one smokes a cigarette and then beats their spouse."

I don't know about the theology in that logic, but that was it for me. That was all the validation I needed. From then on, I handed out the rest of those cigarettes. It took years to get through those cartons. I felt bad giving out packs to people, in case they didn't have self-control, so I gave out a loosie to anyone who wanted one. But that morning, I had none to give to this man. He was maybe 50 and had the look of a man who had not slept well in a while.

The city was sweltering that week. The heavy air made it very difficult to sleep at night. Even the nights were in the 80s and humid. NYC humidity brings out all the smells. Urine, trash, and body odor waft up from the pavement and then linger in the air with nowhere to go but the open windows of restless sleepers.

Moving on from me, the man stumbled through the train car and people pulled their feet back. No one wants to be touched these days. Everyone is hesitant. In NYC during this pandemic most everyone knows someone who has died...I know five people who have passed away.

Upon arriving at Penn Station there is a young man, nearing 30 years old, wearing work boots and a hard helmet waiting to get on the A train. Obviously, he's coming to the city from the burbs on a train to Penn Station where he switched to the local line. I'm sure he is to work on some "essential" construction project hoping to not catch anything to take home to his family. Is it another "essential" luxury apartment that will sit empty or is it something more prestigious? He is not chatty as I try to engage him.

"Is this the platform for the southbound A?" I ask through a mask which everyone is wearing to protect themselves and others.

"Huh?" he replies.

These masks make for brutal conversations.

"This side is the southbound A?" I almost scream.

"Oh yeah," he says lowering his mask. He takes a sip of a Dunks coffee. "All the way downtown," he says in a clearly New Jersey accent. And then he looks back and ahead at nothing, his mask now serving as a chin strap.

There is another man talking a little too loudly to himself. I play that little game where you try to guess what's happening. He is talking to a voice only he can hear; is it pumped in through EarPods or does it exist only in his head? The sweatpants and New Balance scream person who sleeps on the street, but the slight turn of his head reveals the earpiece. This is streetwear, baby. He bounces along by me. The rhythm of his gait matching the tone of his voice. A delightful cadence normally, but at 7:00 a.m. on a Monday, a definite sign of an unbalanced mind, also known as a morning person. His smile and laugh are infectious, but his lack of a mask make people back away as he approaches.

The man asking for change addresses the loud talking man. He holds out his cup, jingling the three coins someone dropped in as they rushed to board the train.

"Sorry man, I don't got nothing for ya."

With that, the first man shuffled off and exited at the next station. He also had on New Balance but a different model and his shoes showed the effects of sleeping rough.

I change trains and get on the F. There are fewer people on this train as it heads out to Brooklyn. I get to the job 15 minutes early, but two of the five movers are already there.

One is Gennero. He is from Naples. "The tough part of Italy," he tells me. He is maybe 6'5" and built like Gru, the oversized cartoon character from the movie Despicable Me. Big, barrel chested, bald head, a big man who clearly skipped both arm-and-leg-day at the gym. But I would learn later, Gennero is plenty strong.

Along with him is Simmons, our driver today. This is a cash business, and I don't know anyone's full name. If the IRS ever comes sniffing around no one even knows anyone's last name to squeal. Additionally, the owner Alex, went through a phase where he would give everyone nicknames. In what would surely be another wrinkle for the IRS, the first names we do know are not their real names. Simmons is not Simmons' name. He has been nicknamed Simmons cause he always looks a little sleepy, so he's Simmons Beautyrest or Simmons for short. Simmons is from the south. Georgia to be exact, his voice reminds me of a recording of a speech I once heard of the author William Faulkner. While Simmons' accent isn't the same as Faulkner's, it sounds close. His voice has a slow cadence, is relaxed, and has a habit of trailing off at the end of each sentence like…

After waiting a while for our missing coworkers, Simmons turned to me and Gennero and said, "Well, I'll go inside and take a look at the inventory." His voice trailed off and I waited to see if there was more. There wasn't. He turned to go inside.

After 10 minutes he reemerged, un-rushed.

"Well it's 8:00 a.m. What do you want to do?" he asked.

I replied, "I mean, we're here, so we may as well get started."

I don't know why I said that. We were being paid by the hour. While the other two guys, not here yet, were paid by the job. It would have been smarter to wait, but I've always been impatient, especially at my own expense apparently. In this job, some guys are paid by the hour and others by the job. Oddly enough the hourly guys were here, while the guys who got paid by the job (and would make triple the amount) were not. It is a convoluted system and when I asked who to talk to so I can better understand it, I was told "you're new, you're going to get the s*** jobs."

Ok, well thank you for that bit of knowledge Captain Obvious. No further questions at this time.

All the same, the masks go back on and we started. We began with the boxes. Mismatched sizes and shapes. There was a surfboard that could not have gotten much use in the middle of Park Slope Brooklyn.

The point man, or boss Nicho, showed up 30 minutes late after we had loaded most of the boxes. "Sorry I'm late," he said. That was it, if we were expecting an explanation or story, "Sorry, I had to deliver a baby on the subway," it was not forthcoming. We were sweaty. It was already in the 80s and humid even that early in the morning. We smiled like a couple greasy mooks. He didn't need our permission to be late. Anyway, it's a two truck job, there are dozens of boxes and heavy furniture to move and that requires effort-- not leadership, we grunts are doing just fine.

One piece, a hope chest was ridiculously heavy which I assumed was filled with precious metals. There was a set of chairs that looked like they could double as cat scratching posts. In the end, if people pay for it to be moved, we move it. Cat posts, fence posts, printed out blog posts, you want them moved, we will move them. The hope chest was a complicated piece, delicate and heavy.

Simmons and I started down the stairs with it and on the last step he slipped on the carpet. My life flashed before my eyes. I mostly saw missed jump shots and not buying Amazon at the IPO -who buys books online? I see Simmons losing his balance and can see that the chest is going to crush him like a grape under a bike tire, getting us both fired if he survives. At the last second, Gennero's giant frame lumbered forward and grabbed the chest and put a protective hand on Simmons.

"Be careful, this can be breaking," he said sounding like an Italian Arnold Schwarzenegger.

After we loaded the truck, the lady of the house offered us popsicles. I took a mango one, savoring the sweet flavor and the momentary cool relief it brought.

We drove through Brooklyn over the Verrazano Bridge to Staten Island. Staten Island began its modern city life as a landfill, making it the most put down and least cool of all the boroughs. It, however, has a certain charm, part of the city but also a very distinct island unto itself. A place so bad, it's good. I have friends who brag about being from the "trash heap." From Staten Island we head to New Jersey, Jersey always greets you with that unique smell as you enter it. Not sure what the smell is, but those refineries put on a nasty little show for your nose. Bottled and marketed as smelling salts would be its only saving grace.

The truck is a 28-foot 2008 snub nose Mitsubishi Sterling. The truck's condition is anything but sterling, it should be named the Mitsubishi Inferior. It has a diesel engine, is automatic with a downshift braking function, but obviously no airbrakes. The biggest problem with these little trucks (other than them losing power going up hills) is that the suspension is quickly destroyed by NYC's roads. Having been driven around on Brooklyn's terrible roads till the wheels fall off means they now bounce around on the highway like little Tonka trucks roughed up by a toddler. The seats have been crushed by big heavy boys for many years and aren't wiped down every week or even every year. No, these seats are crushed and filthy, holding smells of Taco Bell, spilt coffee, and sweat from years of grimy moves.

I quickly learned the AC did not work in any of the trucks, so the driver and one lucky co worker hung an arm out the window, trying to air out at least a part of his body. The poor guy in the middle was left with nothing. He could only stare ahead at the hole in the dash where there used to be a radio and imagine how nice it would be if it was still there. In my mind, the radio is playing George Michael's Careless Whisper, a full saxophone solo romantically droning on as the three of us squish together on this bench seat. The radio was stolen a decade ago and never replaced. Where the radio had been, there was now just a hole with wires sticking out, but it was a perfect analogy for what this truck represented. The abyss. If you're trying to meditate and to clear your thoughts and think of nothing, well here's your chance.This blank space in the dashboard crystallized my thoughts about what I wanted and didn't want for my life. I often stared at that hole and smirked, wondering how my life had taken such a not dark, but strange turn.

I turned to Gennero, "What is Naples like?"

"Beautiful and cheap. We have beautiful countryside." Gennero spoke with an accent so thick it was almost like he was faking it.

"How long have you lived in the states?" I asked.

"Ten years." He replied, eyes fixed forward.

He said he had been here 10 years, but based on his English I would have believed 10 months or perhaps ten hours."Ten years I am here, and still my English is s***." The way he emphasized that last word, I could tell he was disgusted with himself, with his face puckered up. Lips sticking out, he gave a small sideways nod to denote his disgust. "This language. It not so easy. I talk like baby." Maybe, if that baby was a monster. This was a giant man. If he took care of himself, he could definitely play a heel on a wrestling program. He lit up a cigarette without offering us one or asking permission. His long right meat hook hung out the window, extending halfway down the door. Blue smoke swirled around the cab and eventually exited out the window.

Simmons was still driving, right hand holding the wheel at 4:00, left arm hanging out the window without a care in the world. He had the cool two-day stubble on his chin that perfectly balanced the slight male pattern baldness that was starting to creep in up top. He didn't talk much, but he gave off an air of confidence that would have been annoying if I hadn't watched him lugging down the stairs an old trash can and a worn old chair earlier in the day, which would humble anyone's look. It's hard to look cool while doing backbreaking physical labor.

He looked athletic, maybe a diver, though not cliff diving. Simmons is the type of man who would think that sort of sport uncivilized, but Olympic diving, that's where the glory is.

He often had a curious look on his face as if he had just thought of the funniest little ditty but couldn't share it cause you just wouldn't get it. Was it actually that funny? Or was he just recalling that time his brother got hit in the nads with a soccer ball? Hard to tell with him. He's not sharing much.

We bounced along the highway, Gennero talked about Naples.

"You can rent an apartment, one room, $300. You can eat nice restaurant with girl, maybe have a couple drinks, $30." The way he said 30 sounded like he was saying dirty, dirty dollars.

"But now in Italy. No work." He lifts his massive shoulders and his left arm almost hits me in the face. I catch a nice whiff of Old Spice mixed with onions. His face and gestures are so expressive when he talks. He probably could have an entire conversation without using words. He waved his arms so much that, if he'd have stood outside talking, planes would have started to land.

Gennero changing subjects suddenly, "Be good to eat."

Simmons, "Yeah, ok."

Gennero, "There is Wendy's," pointing with an arm long enough to please any grandma's request to reach top shelf items.

"Ok." says Simmons with a twang.

The Wendy's is next to an empty parking lot and the truck slides in with ease.

The masks go back on. Inside, the dining room is roped off. There are stickers on the floor showing people where to line up to order and how far apart six feet is, but still the people ignore them. There is a line of eight people. A man at the front of the line is wearing black socks and plastic slip-on Fila flip flops. He is picking up four different orders for DoorDash. There is a plastic divider between him and the cashier and both are wearing masks. He is having a hard time making himself understood. He speaks with a South East Asian accent and the cashier replies in a Dominican accent. Separated by a common language. Eventually he receives his order and leaves. The next person starts to order. Back in the store comes Flip Flop Fila.

"No nuggets in order 3!" He says through the plastic divider while wearing a mask.

"Snow stuck in Oregon tree?" is the reply from the other side of the plastic divider. How could that possibly be? Snow? How could he honestly think that's what he said?

"No nuggets in order 3!" Flip Flops says yelling now. It sounds less angry and more an issue of comprehension and trying to overcome the barrier.

"No nuggets! You should have said that," the cashier says without a hint of irony.

We get our food and head back to the truck. I order some sort of southwest salad, which turns out to be a mistake. Simmons wanted to wait in the sweltering truck. He also didn't want us to get him anything as he packed a lunch. When we reach him in the truck he is almost finished. He is eating out of a Tupperware container with a real fork. It was some sort of faro, mixed with maybe tofu, arugula, avocado and some things I can't figure out. When we get there, he closes it up and puts it behind the seat.

We climb in. Gennero says, "It-is-very-hot,"as if he is narrating our lives for a movie for the visually impaired. "Now a skinny pink man what's called a Kirk is climbing onto a very hot rubber seat. Then Italian Giant with hunched shoulders and Gumby- like arms climbs in and places this food on his little legs."

Simmons says "Ok," in sort of a singsong reply, and puts the truck in gear. We get back on the highway.

On the road Simmons says nothing but his eyes slowly scan the scenery. Forty more minutes of Gennero's breaking down Naples and Simmons' silence, we arrive. The last 10 minutes are through a residential area where we are limited to 30 miles an hour. At this lower speed, there is no circulation in the truck, even with the windows down. It is now over 90 degrees and the enormous front windshield is roasting us like three poorly aged, greasy rotisserie chickens. I have probably lost five pounds in this hotbox of body odor, Old Spice, stale cigarette smoke, and coffee breath. The coffee breath is my dreary little contribution.

When we finally arrive, I'm sweating profusely, like a Coke in one of those old print ads. Sweat beading up and dripping down my stomach, forming a little puddle with the lint in my belly button. I should sit up straighter; that's what my mom would say and I make an effort to stiffen my back. I'm dying to get out of this truck cab. But I wait for these two to get out first and let me off of this hump in the middle of the cab's hot little bench seat directly over the engine. I act like I don't mind as Gennero slowly unfolds himself like a ladder getting out of a clown car at a glacial pace. He finally moves over, and I hop down out of the cab myself. My legs are both fully asleep from the rhythmic bouncing of the truck. My hips slowly decompress, and I can feel my lower back again. I walk away from the truck looking like a newborn giraffe, each step appearing to be the one that sends me careening to the gravel.

The house is a nice two-bedroom Cape Cod. The lawn is pristine and has what looks like new sod laid down. There are three steps up to the house. Three. Oh yeah. After walking furniture down five flights of stairs, three steps make me just giddy with excitement. It isn't until we get inside that we notice the interior stairs. It is only a two story, but the ceiling in the staircase comes down low, very low. Gennero will have to duck his head.

The unload is smooth. It's always smoother than the load. There is less to do and unwrapping is faster than wrapping.

Gennero is deceivingly strong. Most of these guys are. My guess is the grind of constantly lifting pushes their bodies to adapt, requiring them to get as much as possible out of their physiques. There were a few men with abs and a very few who looked like underwear models, but their bodies were functional and could lift. The weaker and more prone to injuries were weeded out naturally. This moving company hires a lot of artists. Sculptors and welders tend to do well, poets usually don't last. That 7:00 a.m. alarm clock is brutal, and any excuse is enough to get some to quit. Also, the benefits suck, so if you could do something else that pays close to the same, do it, obviously. This job has no disability insurance, no 401k or company beer and pizza parties. What it does have is cash. Big sweaty handfuls of cash at the end of the day that you're welcome to buy pizza with. Honestly, you can eat anything you want as you're probably going to burn it off. At least that's what we tell ourselves and that's also why most of us have those little pot bellies, like we are expecting in the fall.

"Is it a boy or a girl?"

"Ahh, it's a chicken burrito, half a pepperoni pizza from Paulie Gee's and a Reeses Peanut Butter Cup. Also are you going to finish that hotdog?"

After the unload, we stand around looking sheepishly while Simmons squared the bill. This is when the tip is decided. This is what makes the job. If the job has a lot of stairs or is in sweltering heat, it's all good if the tip is generous. If the tip is a little light, it makes the drive back brutal. I could have stayed home and navel gazed or perused Reddit's incels for the next hot stock tip.

I hate tipping, both the giving and the receiving. It feels like a weird leftover custom from an earlier time where something had to be added at the end because the pay structure was broken. Giving a tip is not fun. I just want it included in the price so that I give the right amount. But receiving a tip is just as bad. Here we are, three grown men, sweating after a full day of work, waiting hat in hand, to see if we are worthy of a wage that can support a family in this crazy city. NYC is especially unique in being able to keep afloat a whole insular moving industry. So many people come every day with a dream, but leave when they either make it or are broken by this expensive city. I loathe being paid by tip. However, if you're going to tip the waiter or waitress for carrying your food five steps, tip the guy carrying your whole kitchen and stove down five flights of stairs into a truck, driving it 50 miles and carrying it back up more stairs to the new kitchen.

Today the tip is solid and Gennero starts nodding silently when we get it. We say our thank yous and goodbyes and pile back into the cab, which is now well over 100 degrees. But it doesn't matter, life is good.

Gennero says, "This is what I am talking about. You can't do this in Naples. No way, not possible. There no jobs like this. I was electrician, it pay…" he doesn't finish the sentence but blows a raspberry. Yeah, that's what you do in a pandemic, spit it all out, bud. I close my eyes, partly in tiredness, but mostly to keep the spit particles out of my eyes. Gennero prattles on for another 30 minutes and then, "I have to make piss, stop somewhere."

I am 11 hours into my day, it's almost 6 p.m. We still need to take all the blankets back to the company storage and lock up the truck. I will be getting home after 8 p.m. tonight. But if Gennero can be grateful for his new start, and new job in a new country, I can be grateful, too. Today was a good day, we worked hard, no one got hurt and we are almost home safely.

Simmons silently pulls over at a gas station. We all get out. As we walk slowly towards the gas station, stiffly like a trio of filthy cowboys, Simmons looks like he is going to finally say something.

"Well," Simmons says. Gennero and I lean our heads in to hear his first full sentence of the day. "I'll tell you one thing about this job. It sure gives you a lot of boogers."

"What?" I reply.

"I said, you get a lot of boogers in this job."

I thought that's what he said. I had hoped I heard wrong. I hadn't. No mention of me being fired, just boogers; apparently I'm back again tomorrow. Gennero and I look at him blankly. That is not what we thought he was going to say. I guess Simmons is thankful for the boogers, the important thing is to be thankful.

It's better to stay quiet and be thought a fool than open your mouth and remove any doubt.

Weak Back Strong Mind

Not to brag, but I have been a son all my life, and I have a dad. So, you would think that I would know how to be a dad. How hard can it be? My best friend in high school was a father twice before we graduated (and grandad before he was 30, but that's a different story.) To be a dad, you just do what your dad did, avoiding the obvious mistakes that require you to have therapy now.

But getting along with your parents and being a parent are not always straightforward.

And being a parent is thankless, confusing and never ending.

When I used to lift heavy things with my dad, he used to encourage me by saying, "You can do it! You have a weak mind, but a strong back," which was funny as it was the opposite of what I both had and wanted. As a kid, my dad pushed me in sports. Our bond over sports was one of the few moments I remember holding his interest as a child, which ultimately sparked my enthusiasm about their importance. When I was three, I ran my first race. My parents were racing, and I said I wanted to run, so they let me enter. I wanted the attention, I guess. I assume I trained how all three - year -olds train: finger painting, drinking too much apple juice and running to the bathroom. Did I have a passion for the sport? I was three, I had a passion for macaroni necklaces, trying to remember my own name and to wear clothes. With no training or passion for the sport, I finished the race, last place, and made the paper. Years later, I don't remember any of it, but my dad kept the newspaper clipping and beams even now if it comes up. There's my picture in the paper, shirtless and running. I was slow, but I finished; a perfect metaphor for me. Sports were a straightforward, if not always easy way, to get attention. I've heard it said that people end up comedians if they have not been hugged enough, or if they have been hugged too much. I am in the latter camp.

When I turned 12, I discovered basketball. We lived in Guayaquil and I was almost six feet tall, which is pretty tall in the 1980s in America, but positively Gulliverian in Ecuador. My dad had installed a hoop in our back yard where he would work on his three-point shot. He was always a big proponent of the three-point shot.

Draining three-point shots from the top of the key he explained his love of the three-pointer. Where he played pickup basketball, they played ones and twos, meaning "See, each 2-pointer is worth one, and each 3-pointer is worth 2! So, it's worth 100% more, it's double. You only have to make it 30% of the time from the 3-point line to equal someone else shooting 60% for 2!" There is no way around it: he is a numbers guy. Even when it came to sports, my dad thought practically and in terms of numbers. As a 12-year-old I didn't know much, but I knew that 2 was more than 1. I cared less about winning and more about not losing– I definitely didn't want to lose.

Guayaquil is on the coast of Ecuador, and we used to call it the armpit of South America. Directly on the equator, it is hot, humid and stinky. I never cared for the oppressive humidity Guayaquil offered. The unrequested sauna whenever I would venture outside meant I would sweat through my clothes just sitting on a public bus. While playing basketball I would turn into a living puddle making smaller billabongs all over the asphalt we played on. While a sloppy mess, I found I was serviceable as an athlete as long as I didn't touch anything that needed to stay dry.

My dad also had a regular basketball game every Saturday at 7:00 a.m. When I was suddenly a few inches taller than him, he allowed me to come and play. We started the games early to avoid the heat. I have never been a morning person, but sports was the exception. -During these first few games with my dad, I wandered around the court, like a lost single white sock mixed in with the darker laundry, unsure of where to stand or what to do. As I mostly did nothing on the court, the guy guarding me would get bored and occasionally leave me to go double team someone good; when he would leave me, I would raise my hands and run under the basket. If they passed me the ball, I would shoot. My motto: "Wait till they forget about me, and then shoot it," while my team yelled, "Don't screw it up!"

With practice, I slowly improved. I started practicing the shots that I knew I would get, which were primarily directly under the hoop, shooting straight up at the basket. My dad was a natural coach and always gave me new shots to practice. One of the things I have liked most about basketball was seeing the tangible results. For weeks, I worked on a shot, then eventually perfected it and introduced it in a game. Seeing improvements was a powerful motivator for me to continue practicing my game in the Ecuadorian heat. There was a direct correlation between the work I put in and positive results, usually. On the other hand, building muscle was a different story.

I was a very slight boy with the muscle tone of a wordsmith, not a blacksmith. Nutrition wasn't really a consideration back then. What we focused on was a little bit of running, weight training, and pushups. But I constantly looked like the before picture for a nutritional supplement. "Try our new chocolate flavored Youza powder, so you don't have to look like this loser!" (Insert picture of me smiling like a buffoon.) I did my best, but you can't get blood from a stone.

The last 10 years have brought many changes. A short while ago I lived a much different life. I was married with two kids, working a normal job. Then we separated. My wife decided she wanted to live in Sri Lanka, and not with me. A short time after that I was widowed. After multiple attempts, the woman I had been married to for 17 years took her own life and it hit me hard. In some instances, when it rains, it pours. My daughter got married against my advice, and my severely disabled son, now a man, moved into an assisted-living home. The facility unfortunately banned visitors during the pandemic, limiting our frequent visits to short video calls on most mornings. And because misery loves company, standup comedy, which I had worked at for well over a decade, stopped altogether. All of the clubs, venues, and cruise ships closed indefinitely. All of them. For how long? No one knows.

So, in a moment of genius or madness I took a job as a mover with my strong back, weak mind.

The company was called Fierce Movers, which would only be appropriate if they meant Fiercely Disorganized Movers. Or perhaps Fierce Ex-con Movers, of which we had our fair share. The man who hired me was named Carlos. He looked like an exaggerated version of a homeless person with shifty eyes and many noticeable spaces in the front of his mouth where teeth used to be. The rumor was that he was mainly a drug dealer, why he would want to mess with a moving business during his off-drug hours is beyond me. Maybe this is like CrossFit for chubby drug peddlers. "Do you want to get in shape but resent having to wear clean work out clothes to the gym? Come work out at Fierce Movers! Here you can work out in jeans and a stained t-shirt that you have had 15 years that has the smell of ammonia that never comes out! Want to get into a weekly shouting match with a parking attendant that looks sure to escalate into violence? You've come to the right place, you're home!"

During our first meeting Carlos said, "Hey Kirk," and then eyed me up and down the way you look at bad supermarket meat. He paused, "I bet you drive, don't you?" I guess my athletic shorts with zippered pockets and sleeveless shirt gave me away.

Me, "Yeah, I drive."

Carlos, "Great, you'll drive tomorrow." And that was it. After 10 minutes explaining how to wrap furniture and another glance at me, I was in. "You'll learn the rest on the job," Carlos told me before disappearing. Where did he go? I don't know, maybe to have that enormous stain removed from a mid 90s Boston Celtics shirt he was wearing but should throw away.

No one ever asked to look at my driver's license. No one took a photocopy of it. No one asked if I had a DUI. I guess it was all taken on faith that a formerly athletic man with basketball shorts, a long tailed black T-shirt, and old Adidas can maneuver a moving truck with no training.

The first person I helped move was a doctor. How do I know that? Because she told us. Again and again.

My coworker Noah gives me the address of the move, and nothing else. I confirm and tell him that I am stopping at Dunks on the way, offering to buy him something. "Black coffee," he texts back. I stop at Dunks for a black coffee and get myself a large iced coffee. That later proved to be a near disastrous mistake. A few moments later, I locate the 28-foot truck on the corner of St. Nicholas and Flushing. This truck is an innocuous white, with most of the front right wheel well missing from an unfortunate event with a guard rail. The keys were locked inside the rear of truck with a combination lock placed on the rollup door. The combination is the same for all the trucks, 2023. That number unlocks all the trucks in the fleet. It has been that number for years now. I fully expect one day to hear that a truck is stolen by some disgruntled former employee.

One day I will be told: -"Someone stole one of our trucks, can you believe it?"

Me: "One of the trucks which have the keys locked inside them overnight? One of the trucks with a combination lock on it that is known by literally hundreds of ex-cons who are also ex-employees and hate the owner? Wow super weird, that would have been impossible to predict, unless you know, you thought about it for one second."

We called the doctor the night before to confirm the move but she didn't pick up. All the same, we showed up bright and early at her place at 9:00 a.m. That meant leaving my house at 7:00, to get to the truck at 8:00 in Brooklyn, to be in Mt. Vernon by 9:00 a.m.

Noah introduces himself to me. He is a young Jewish kid from Jersey. He is also dating a doctor, but not the lady we are moving. "Yeah, she's not Jewish, but she's a doctor… that's close enough for my parents," he tells me on the drive up to the move.

I get into the truck and realize my athletic shorts, black T-shirt, and scuffed Adidas have not prepared me for driving this 28-foot long, box truck entrusted to my care. This is big. The truck is a Ford with only fifteen thousand miles on the odometer, but the exterior is beaten as if it was driven through Armageddon by a teenager with a fake learner's permit. The graffiti on the sides of the truck is rather crass, yet beautifully done. Turning the keys in the ignition, I slowly back up out of a tight spot the prior driver had parked in the night before and get it out on the road. In New York, there are archaic rules about trucks being allowed on freeways but not parkways. Meaning, we have to figure out how to get to Mt. Vernon (NY, not George Washington's old stomping grounds) on city streets and eventually highways. We arrive at the client's location a few minutes late.

It's been about two hours since I drank that coffee on an empty stomach.

Me: "I'm going to have to drop a deuce."

Noah: "Oh, that's going to be a problem. Number One Rule at Fierce Movers is, no s***ing at the client's home."

That's the number one rule? Not checking to see if the new guy has a license before asking him to drive a 28-foot truck through Brooklyn? Or checking that he doesn't sell drugs on the side? Also, that information would have been helpful when I handed you the coffee I bought you this morning. But it's my first day, so I keep these thoughts to myself.

"We'll find some place later on," he says.

NYC is mostly shut down and there are very few bathrooms available. Earlier that morning, I had asked to use the bathroom at Dunks but they said it was closed. Before that, when I drove to pick up the truck, I had stopped at McDonald's but got the same answer, no bathrooms.

I smile and say nothing. This is going to be a long day.

I hope the expression has evolved to "weak back, strong mind and bowels."

The lady we are helping today is moving to Oceanside Long Island and is keen to detail all the places she plans on leisurely drinking in her new domain. We try to listen between trips down to the truck with her things. She was working as an ER doctor for the last 25 years and is now retiring to Oceanside.

"If things go as planned, I won't have a sober day the rest of my life," she crows to us. That's an unusual goal, but you're in luck. Alcohol is sold literally everywhere in this country, from bars to supermarkets and in NYC, even at Taco Bell. Not sure if you pair red or white wine with a chalupa. Which wine pairs better with indigestion and upset stomach?

The move is done. It was a physically and mentally exhausting uninspiring first day, I already know this job will be unforgiving on both the body and the spirit. The newly retired, tired, and already tipsy MD(I think she will achieve her goal) pulled out two envelopes. After being paid and saying our goodbyes, we get back into the truck to do the post-move math: half for the company, subtract the tolls, add in the additional assembly of the bed cost, then divide up the tip.

The drive home from Oceanside is gridlock and I think of my dad and our nights perfecting our 3-point shots in Guayaquil. He would use any excuse to practice math and numbers.

"You shot 3 for 8. What percent is that?"

I do one of the quick calculation tricks he taught me, half of 8 would be 4, which would be 50%. Three is less than 4, so the answer has to be less than 50; how much less, I don't know -- a little.

"40%?" I guess.

"Yeah close, maybe 38%?" my dad says, offering it as if he doesn't already know the answer.

Sometimes, it's easier to just memorize a few math answers, you'd be surprised at how much they come up.

Noah is asking me something and my mind shoots back to the present.

"For the tip she just rounded up the bill to $1300 from $1211. So that's $89.?" he says reading the numbers off of the calculator app on his phone.

"So, the tip is like $35. each?" he continues.

"Yeah, I think so, like $44.50 each," I agree. That's another $44.50 towards JJ's car.

And that is why I have always loved math, because there is an answer. There is a solution. There is a right and there is a wrong. In my experience, life is not like that. It is rarely that clean cut, you make your best guess, smile and keep moving forward.

That's what parenting is like. When your kids are born you think, "Oh wow, how am I the parent? There must be a mistake, I know nothing. This is the blind leading the blind." I have made a lot of mistakes as a son and as a father. I'm sure this realization would make my dad smile.

I can almost hear him say, "Not as easy as it seems, is it? But you can do it!" from somewhere deep in the sweaty part of Ecuador.

Bridge Over Troubled Water

"Yeah, I went to school. I have a master's degree in creative writing, what a waste," is what I heard Wilfred say before he continued. "Whatever, I just started over. I mean, I guess that's the American way." Yep, 70 thousand dollars in debt on a degree that you're not using and living with three roommates who are slowly driving you crazy, that's the American way. I would give my right arm to have a degree in creative writing, but I don't know if I would give 70k. He tells me about growing up in Seattle and his seasonal depression disorder.

We are one hour into a 13-hour workday and are inching our way across the Williamsburg Bridge. Traffic is heavy and I am asking him questions about his life just hoping to fill the time before we have to lift more heavy objects into a heavily tagged box truck.

He is from Seattle but has been in NYC for eight years. He has the disgusted, antagonistic edge and tone of a man twice his age. He is angry at the traffic, at his buddy who got him this job and at the truck. He is like Bert from Bert and Ernie only a slightly less pointy head. He is in his early thirties and in great shape.

Having three roommates when you're in your early thirties is distressing in most cities. In NYC, where a 3 bedroom might rent for $4,000 a month, three guys living together is semi-normal. Perhaps not desirable or preferred, but understandable especially if there is an economic downturn and people are trying to keep costs down and just looking for a bridge to happier times.

From the Williamsburg Bridge, you can catch a quick glimpse of the Manhattan and Brooklyn Bridges, and a beautiful view of the NYC skyline. It's 7:30 a.m. and the sun is rising in the east and shining down on the city, a small fog is lifting off of the buildings. It's my favorite time of the day. The city is coming alive and possibilities are all around us.

While Brooklyn Bridge gets all the love, the bridge from Williamsburg is my favorite. It's the more anonymous sibling. Working class, functional, but far from flashy and famous.

Wilfred is wearing a hat and athletic gear. His shirt is made of the Dri-Fit material that wicks away moisture, but also stubbornly refuses to completely wash away the odor of sweat. After a dozen wears, the bacteria build-up is intense and this shirt smells like it's been hanging in an Alabama outhouse. We met for the first time today.

This truck is covered in graffiti, absolutely every square inch. All of the trucks have graffiti from the same artist. The artist's name is Cernesto and is relatively famous in NYC. He uses the trucks as murals and has drawn incredible scenes on them. He got permission from the owner to use the vehicles as canvases. The problem is that every other local graffiti artist and gang member who is not nearly as talented as Cernesto has assumed permission also and mercilessly tagged all of our trucks with absolutely anything. The more phallic or profane, the better. No idea is too idiotic or nonsensical. A crossed-eyed rabbit holding a gun? Check. A specific threat to a someone named Jose in the neighborhood? You got it. A cartoon of a naked women? Sure, no matter how impossibly voluptuous her body is shaped. (Can someone's bones even support someone that top heavy?) And once the flood gates are opened, they are hard to close. This truck has probably five layers of "art"painted on it, one on top of the other. Disembodied hands from previous drawings awkwardly linger next to a new addition by a local hooligan.

I got a call from Andy the night before, on a Tuesday at 8 p.m. to tell me about the Wednesday job. "Hey, tomorrow it's a two-truck job. I'm thinking of taking home one truck to Manhattan and then you just pick up T30 (Truck 30) in Brooklyn."

"That's fine," I reply. Andy got me this job and I appreciate it. What he is asking is irregular and technically, he is not allowed to, but again he got me this job. While he is not supposed to be taking the trucks home, he does not work for me, and he is not really asking, he's telling me. He lives in

Manhattan, so me picking up the truck in Brooklyn and him taking home the other truck saves him an hour.

He continues. "Text Justin and ask him where he'll park T30 tonight and then coordinate the meet up with Wilfred. That way, he can drive up to the job with you," Andy says. Today is going to be a 4-man load job. After the load, we'll release one of the workers, and the remaining three of us will drive upstate for the delivery and unload. I had heard about Wilfred from Andy. He is one of Andy's friends from Seattle. Andy had previously told me, "I like to get my friends jobs, but I don't always like to work with them. I like them, but just ...don't want to work with them. Wilfred gets too grumpy and it wears me down. Plus, it's hard to be the boss of your friend." So that's why he wants to hand him off to me. It's going to be a fun ride upstate.

Andy adds, "Also, I have added Lanza to the job, we are going to need him. It's a 4th floor walk-up." Lanza has a beard that is 18 inches long. I have never seen his face, as it is always covered in that mess of whiskers. I worked with him last month on a 2nd floor job, I met him at the top of the stairs to grab a box from him. He had tried to hand me a large, heavy box that he was holding against his chest. Unbeknownst to me, his beard was trapped against his chest as well. Taking the box, I ended up with a fist full of whiskers and attempted to pull his face down the stairs with the box to the truck on the street below. His eyes got wide and he yelped, "Wait, wait, wait," with a childlike energy as he steadied himself on the railing. That's how I learned what Lanza looked like (a stand-in for the guitarist for ZZ Top, complete with the disheveled beard), but I did not yet know what Wilfred looked like.

I ask Andy, "Ok. Hey, what does Wilfred look like, so I'll recognize him?"

Andy says, "He's Asian and is 5'2"."

"Ok," I reply. Well, that's odd. This is one of the few jobs where height and size are an advantage. Normally, being tall is not helpful at all. What are the real advantages? What are we, sword fighting? The only obvious advantage of being tall is that you can reach things on high shelves for old ladies and for that, the tradeoff is you can't fit in many cars or airplane seats, and have a hard time finding pants that can cover your ankles. Doesn't matter, maybe he has strength disproportionate with his body like the Rhinoceros beetles that can carry multiple times their body weight.

I text Justin and ask where T30 is going to be for tomorrow. Flushing and Stewart, 20 minutes from my house, got it. I lay out my clothes and pack my little backpack.

Protein cookies
Water
Charger
Two clean t-shirts
Mask
Dry socks
Salt packs
I learned to pack salt packs at the beginning of this job. I was sweating profusely for hours and started getting headaches by the end of the day. I experimented with salt. If I took a salt pack about four hours into the day and again about eight hours, no headache. It was like magic.

I'm ready for a day of glamour and adventure.

I wake up at 6:30 a.m. to a text from Justin.

"Hey man, there is a crash or something and my ETA keeps going up... can you get my rental, it's T8 on Jefferson and St. Nick and drive it to your job? I will meet you there with this truck."

Well, this is frustrating as it will add an hour to my day, but again, he's not really asking. He's telling. That is the thing. When you're new, they just tell you what to do. I confirm and then have to reach out to Wilfred and Lanza with the new instructions. They are displeased.

"Bro, I'm riding a bike," Wilfred texts me back.

"I'm sorry man, I just got the info from Justin," I tell him, and he doesn't respond. I am guessing he has already put the phone away and is peddling his little legs.

I arrive at the truck and see Lanza's beard there, next to Lanza's bike. Next to him is a man I don't recognize, but he's definitely not 5'2". Maybe 5'11".

"Hey Kirk, I'm Wilfred," he says and extends his fist out for a bump, the new official handshake. Well, that's weird, maybe he had a growth spurt since Andy's text but I don't want to open with, " I thought you were shorter?"

I open the back and grab the key. I unlock the cab door and Wilfred opens the passenger side at the same time. There are only two bucket seats. Wilfred turns to Lanza and says, "Well, you're riding in the back, buddy." They had already placed their bikes on packing blankets in the back. We opened the back gate and Lanza gets in, stepping around blankets and the bikes and reclines on some other blankets.

"Sorry, buddy," I offer. I honestly felt bad for him. I get car sick and riding around in the back of a box truck on NYC's broken roads sounds like a recipe for nausea or disaster. But Lanza seems fine with it. I have worked with him several times and he only has said a few sentences to me. His response to my condolences is a shrug and a look of indifference on his face.

We wind through Brooklyn, starting on Flushing Boulevard and continuing to Queens Boulevard. On the show Entourage, they love to shout out that they're from "Queens Boulevard" like it's somehow cool. I don't know what it used to be, but I know what it is now. It's a pedestrian boulevard filled with franchise chain stores, nothing to get too excited about, and certainly nothing to shout out repeatedly while wearing tacky Affliction t-shirts. It would be like if someone from Dallas yelled out "Oak Park strip mall!" Huh, ok.

We arrive at the client's apartment building, and I see the truck we were supposed to have, parked right out front. Then I see Justin's lumbering figure moving towards me. "Hey man, thanks for getting the truck, you are a lifesaver," he says giving my arm a hard swat.

"You got it bud," I reply and say nothing of the rant that I endured from Wilfred on the way over regarding the change. I let Lanza out of the back and switch keys with Justin.

It's still early and there is commercial parking on this street which is a real gift. There is a slight sprinkle, which I hope will clear the humidity. Some of the trees are shedding flowers and the windshield wipers have captured several petals in the few moments we have been here.

Andy's vape pen has a distracting blue light at the end of it. He takes a long pull, looking pensive, like a tormented Dutch artist, but from the year 2050. He blows the vapor out and then furrows his brow, "Kirk, you watch the trucks. We will go up and start the unload. No tickets today," he lowers his head when he says that last part.

I am not sure if the meter maids in NYC are working under a ticket quota, but almost every company truck has gotten a ticket this week. It is like they are trying to make up for lost time. Perhaps the city is broke and they are trying to fund it, one $100 ticket at a time. Last week, I got a ticket while being in the back of the truck. We were double parked, so technically we deserved it. However, normally we are not ticketed when the driver is actually in or on the truck. All the same, we got it and we had to split the fine, which is a pain in the rear end and lowers the overall money we can take home that day. One ticket equals 50 dollars less for JJ's car.

The furniture and boxes begin to descend on dollies. Big boxes, little boxes, end tables and coffee tables. Then come the bags. There are dozens. This job was not supposed to have bags, but the bags are coming. Black trash bags converted to garment bags. Overstuffed, white, kitchen trash bags with shoes trying to escape through the rips. A homemade hope chest. A carved wood column. The metal circular IKEA table that everyone thinks is unique but is included in every other move this summer. Some bookshelves with nails protruding out the back. Tilting slightly, the rectangular bookcases become parallelograms with the slightest touch. I painstakingly load the truck. The hodgepodge of disjointed items that don't easily stack take up more space than I would like in the back of this dinged-up truck bed. I catch my hand on one of the nails—that is going to leave a mark. The hours tick away, and finally Andy comes down from the walk-up and takes a long drag on his vape that looks like a robot's finger.

I ask him something that had been puzzling me, "You told me Wilfred was Asian and 5'2". He's like 5'11."

He laughs and replies, "I said he's Asian and tattooed." Kirk's deafness has struck again.
He continues, "This job has a second pickup location where we need to get a bed. I'm going to go up there with the other truck and get it and I will meet you guys at the drop off," and with that, he's off. We were left to pack the rest.

We eventually wrap up the load job with four tomato plants and Wilfred's bike in the back. Who moves tomato plants? Us that's who. Lanza will not be coming with us. We say our goodbyes and I pay him his portion of the move as instructed. Technically, I'm advancing him cash, as none of us have yet been paid.

The load had been at 165 Eldridge St. on the Lower East Side. I drove the truck north on Eldridge to Houston and then east to Houston to First Ave., and then again north on First Ave. Commercial traffic as you now know, is not allowed on most of the FDR Drive. The FDR runs on the outer eastern edge of Manhattan at the water's edge which is the fastest way north out of the city, but we are relegated to city streets. Normally, First Ave. is packed, but today with the pandemic, it is light. We pass people pounding their feet on the pavement, moving almost in unison to their destinations. There are no tourists during this time of restricted travel, so there are no people walking slowly on the sidewalk staring up at the buildings in awe. Instead, the passersby are staring robotically straight ahead or down at their phones.

We are moving north on First Ave. passing Veniero's, that favorite local with its insane pastries. Mt. Sinai Beth Israel comes up on the left, and then the massive NYC Hospital on the right. The constant stream of ambulances headed to these hospitals during the early months of COVID-19 has slowed to a crawl. The historic landmarks blur past us, one by one. We pass by the UN General Assembly Building on the right at 42nd street. Consulates as varied as Germany and Thailand whiz by. First Ave has two Catholic Hungarian Churches. St. John Nepomucene comes up on the east side at 66th street, a 130-year-old Catholic church started by Slovaks, with a Hungarian name but not to be confused with another Catholic Hungarian church, The Parish of St. Monica and St. Elizabeth 20 some odd blocks up at 79th street. The latter was constructed 10 years earlier, also Catholic, also Hungarian, and a true Gothic beauty. And finally, we're within a block of Asphalt Green, where weekend warriors, like myself come out to try to stave off the fat for one more year. Then on to Harlem, and through the Bronx. In the Bronx we pass a basketball game in the park. There is a shout up from players. We obviously just missed a great play and there is no replay in real life. Pay attention. If you didn't see it, it's gone forever. You just keep moving forward. We make it to the freeway that is littered with billboards and blacktop patches.

I wonder if the client also took this scenic route, having one last taste of NYC before moving off to the suburbs and exchanging this vibrance for peace and silence.

We drive north to Highland, NY. Highland is a small town of five thousand people located on the West bank of the Hudson River. The client is renting a house there for a year or two. But not just any house. This is a house built by Joseph Caroff, an artist born a hundred years ago. He lived almost as long. He created almost 300 film campaigns, including Westside Story, Barbarella, and the famous original James Bond logo. He was a B-17 armorer in the 8th Army Air Force who also designed the propaganda leaflets that were dropped on Europe in the Second World War, as well as the famous, scantily clad women that adorned the B-17s. What was considered scantily clad 80 years ago can be posted on facebook by grandmas now. Times change.

We ramble north up 87, an unremarkable highway with none-the-less beautiful greenness at the pavement's edges. We eventually veer off onto old Route 9W until finding Red Top Road, which the house is on. At the first attempt to find the house, we missed it completely. At the road's edge is an old barn from the last century— standing, but just barely. Having survived two world wars and now, two pandemics, it is resilient. It might outlive me, but this barn couldn't be the house. Next to the barn is a gravel road and we could see that it winds through the trees. This had to be our next route. The road less traveled.

We turn on this gravel trail headed towards the Hudson River. The tires slowly turn on the gravel, kicking up odd stones from time to time. Two hundred yards from the paved road, the house comes into view. It is painted a sky blue and the design is strongly influenced by Frank Lloyd Wright. Low pitched roofs, a streamline design, the epitome of modern when created. Built in 1985, it beckons to an earlier esthetic, well-lit by enormous windows, and blending in with the surrounding nature. The house is beautiful.

We were instructed that the key for the house would be left under a stone beside the front door. Indeed, it is. We open the house and confirm that the living room, that we noticed through the bay window, is a perfect place to start unloading items. There is a staircase on the right side of the living room that is held up with climbing ropes. A brilliant little piece of ingenuity. I later painfully discover that a full staircase can be lowered from the ceiling in the living room. The design is similar to a ladder that is lowered to access an attic. This staircase can be lowered with a series of pulleys. Remarkable and gorgeous. We begin to unload before the client or Andy arrive; a third of the truck is unloaded by the time they do.

The client, who's named Paul, pulls up in a lowered Volkswagen GTI with rims that cost more than my whole car. It's a beautiful ride that will be incredibly ill-suited to northeast winters on gravel roads. Flash and fast, the opposite of the direction he has decided to take his life, in this soon to be winter wonderland.

"I haven't even seen this place yet!" Paul exclaims as he bounds up the stairs at the front of the home. "We rented it based off the pictures." He says as if describing buying a doll house.

He and his partner begin to explore their new deluxe residence going from room to room like kids on Christmas. He heads upstairs through the magic stairs and discovers the pull system.

"Oh man! You have to see this babe," he yells down. She pokes her head out from the kitchen and lets out a, "Huh, cool," and goes back to unpacking boxes of dishes and cooking utensils.

Wilfred and I continue to unload the truck, bags, beds, bureaus, backpacks, books, baubles, and bric-a-brac. As I walk back into the house carrying an unnecessarily heavy box, I remember thinking we are 70% done with the first truck. I turn to exit and the next thing I remember, I am lying flat on my back seeing stars and stairs. It took me a second to figure out what happened. As I lie there in Savasana (the only yoga pose I can do), I can see the staircase has been lowered about halfway down and I am lying next to it. This ding-dong has dropped the staircase directly on my head. I would be mad if I wasn't in so much pain.

"Oh my God! I can't believe I did that!" I hear Ding Dong yell from upstairs. "Are you ok?"

I sit up with pounding in my head and check my hand, after rubbing my noggin. No real blood. Well, that's good, no stitches. "Give me a second," I say weakly.

"I'm done playing with that, I can't believe that just happened," Paul has now lowered the stairs completely and is pacing frantically waving his hands around. That didn't "just happen"; he was messing with it while not paying attention and I could have broken my neck.

Wilfred comes over and has a serious look on his face. "Take a few minutes and rest. Are you ok?"

Paul jumps in, "I'm so sorry. I don't like to hit guests in my house with stairs."

His partner, "Seriously Paul. Why?"

Paul walks into the kitchen and they have a hushed argument that we can all hear. I take a little while to answer Wilfred. "Yeah, I need a minute," I manage.

I take a few wobbly steps out the front door rubbing the knot on my head furiously. I sit on the deck steps my head pounding, I think I'm going to throw up.

"I think I'm going to throw up," I say to no one in particular, but Wilfred is already walking inside with a box and he's passing me while I am sitting there.

"Try to, man, that might get us a better tip." Honestly, I can't understand why Andy doesn't want to work with his friend.

I sit for a few minutes and then make my way to the back of the truck. I would rather move around, I think. I pass Andy who is taking a box off the back.

"I'll get on the truck. I'm a little wobbly but I think I can move the stuff from the back of the truck to the edge for you to unload," I say as I climb on the truck.

"Geez, are you still talking about your concussion? What a baby," Andy says in fake distain and rolls his eyes broadly and smiles. Clearly my mom is not on this crew. His comment would be the limit of the attention my near decapitation receives. No one cares.

I get on the truck and start pushing boxes forward. The minutes tick by and we finish this truck and replace it with the other one. We grind the stack down until it is finished.

As I get ready to leave, Paul offers me an icepack for my head which I take and make some dumb joke, so he won't feel so bad. Even now I'm trying to make him feel better about how he made me feel terrible. The tip was ok, but Wilfred is right. Probably not as good as it would have been if I have vomited everywhere.

It is decided that Wilfred will drive the truck down with Andy, so I will be driving the 30 footer down to the rental company alone. I shouldn't be shocked. Why would I be surprised that they've given heavy machinery to a concussed man, when they don't even check essential things.

We say our goodbyes and I pull out of the driveway holding an icepack on my coconut with my right hand, thankful this rig is not a stick-shift. I drive down the country road to the highway, to the bridges. There are a few options to getting back to where I need to drop the truck off. I choose the Williamsburg Bridge.

When this bridge was completed, it had the longest suspension span in the world, and it held the title for barely 20 years. Its cousin up the road soon took it, Bear Mountain. Then the Ben Franklin, the George Washington, the Ambassador, and the Golden Gate held the title for a little while too. The current champion is the Akashi-Kaikyo Bridge, constructed in 1998.

These bridges held title for a hot minute, until a new and improved bridge came along and stripped the old bridge of its glory. A new title holder, younger, stronger, brighter. The former title holder faded into obscurity, like a boxer who failed to defend his title.

"He was the best at one time," someone would say.

"Who are we talking about?" would be the reply.

"I can't remember his name, but he was a heck of a boxer."

Williamsburg is like the Ken Norton of bridges. For a brief moment he was the heavy weight champ of the world. Before Ken Norton's fight with Ali, Sports Illustrated had called Ken Norton "Ken Somebody". Legendary announcer Howard Cosell had said that Norton was a "tailor-made" fall guy for Ali, yet Norton himself believed he could do it. He was given long odds to win but in the end he had the will and determination to go all the way.

Ali was a world class trash talker. He couldn't help himself, and before the fight he had to show up at a training session and call Ken Norton an "amateur". Later that week Ken Norton broke Ali's jaw. In a strange ironic twist, Ali's jaw had to be wired shut.

Norton the former marine, didn't know he was supposed to be scared, so he wasn't. He would get knocked down and but not give up.

In the fight before the Ali fight, his pay had been all of 300 dollars. Three hundred dollars. No one saw him as a real challenge for Ali. He was what's called a tune-up fight, a fight to get Ali ready for the real fight, a rematch with George Foreman.

But Norton didn't know that he didn't have a chance. He believed he did.

Life can be a slippery little mistress. One minute you're on top of the world, the next you're nursing a jaw broken in several places like Ali. And Ali? He came back too and regained the belt again.

The thing is life will always try to knock you down whether you're a prince or a pauper. It may not be a falling staircase on your head, and for your sake, I hope it's not. It may not be with someone breaking your jaw. No, for most people these knockouts come with less publicity or fanfare and in the folds of everyday life. It will be a sudden illness, lost job, or unexpected financial downturn. But when these knockdowns come, and they will, the important thing is to get up with or without grace and keep moving.

When we get knocked onto our butts, heads pounding with pain, it's easy to pity ourselves, wondering if anyone will notice if we give up. But life keeps moving on. It will always move on.

The only real option we have is to keep moving with it. You can do it, it's just life.

My Good Ear

It is raining torrentially this morning and I'm fine with it. We have had a week of rain and thunderstorms in the NYC. The rain has cleared out the humidity and muggy air. It has been oppressively hot lately. Mid 90s which is nothing compared to the deserts of Nevada, but 90s with 80% humidity feels like the devil's arm pit.You can feel the humidity being sucked into the mask and then down into your lungs. It feels thick like a fog machine except without all the fun-house music and glitz.

We three movers have already worked for hours loading household goods onto the truck and are now sitting in the cab on the plastic covered bench seat headed to another location to unload our cargo. We have been assigned T3, a sad little truck, that never had AC. The only reason it has no AC is the guy buying it knew he was never going to drive it. The sun is beaming through the windshield cooking us like three hams. Today, two pink and one brown ham.

We are halfway through unloading the truck at the new place, 180 Manhattan St., which oddly enough is in Jersey City. The house is on a hill and I had to parallel park the truck on a steep incline Although a tight fit, I managed it, and was secretly very proud of that. We have taken all the big things into the house and now we're down to the boxes. Boxes are always the first things into the truck and the last things out. They stack nicely against the back of the cab like wood Alphabet Blocks, packed very tightly, saving much needed space for later. The truck bed is a good four feet off the ground. Between the ground and the truck is a small step sticking out like a lip. I stack two boxes together and lift them trying to remember to use my legs. Use your legs. Use your legs. Everyone who hears I am working as a mover says that to me. I even bought a back belt to save my back. Unfortunately, it is at home, still in its original packaging waiting to be opened.

I step down off the truck onto the metal step. The whole back of the truck is wet, soaked from hours of rain. My foot stays on the step for a half-second and then slips out from under me. The boxes get thrown into the air and I fall face down toward the street. My knees hit the asphalt hard as do my hands and arms. I end up with my face an inch from the ground. Wow. Well, that hurts. As I was falling, I heard myself in an old man voice yell out, "Oh crap," in a singsong resignation of what was coming.

I lie on the ground for a second and can hear the voice of my college basketball coach ringing through my head. My mind flashes back to that moment decades ago when he said those words.

"Well, sweetheart? Are you hurt or are you injured?" At that time, I had just been undercut on a layup and had landed awkwardly on my back having the wind knocked out of me.

"What's the difference?" I weakly said trying to get air back in my lungs.

"If you're injured, something is broken. And you can't play. If you're hurt, you can still play."

"I'm hurt," I say still trying to breathe and squinting as if that somehow helped.

"Well then get up, "he said, turning away. "Run it again, ladies," he then said to all of us.

There were no ladies present. This was a closed gym practice, and we were running plays. I was 20 years old and it was one of the best years of my life despite being flat on my back and unable to breathe.

My mind begins to focus on what's around me now and the pain from my extremities comes shooting back. I'm back in Jersey City, lying face down in a literal gutter. I could feel a shooting pain in my right knee and a dull pain in my left knee. I slowly roll over. Rain is falling on my face. It is August, 75 degrees, and the rain is cool and refreshing. The gutter water is flowing down hill, as it normally would, and is filling my shorts. I try to pull myself to my feet. I hurt. There is intense pain down my right leg and I imagine myself with a pronounced limp for the rest of my life. I wonder what kind of cane I should get? I'm thinking something classy and timeless. Maybe a wooden cane with an exaggerated hook. Oh, maybe I'll get one of those canes that have a sword inside. Or better yet, an umbrella which I could have used today.

The day has been wacky right out of the gate. I was teamed up with PJ again. I don't know how, but I had a premonition that things would not go smoothly. They say you can measure a man by the quality of his enemies, and if PJ is my enemy, I really have accomplished nothing. It's been said, never argue with an idiot; they will drag you down to their level and win with experience.

The rain amusingly put me in a fine mood this morning, until I got to the truck that I thought I had been assigned. It was an old Ford.

I looked at the front license plate. I opened my phone and checked the Google shared document with the number of the truck license plate number. They didn't match. This truck had a different license plate than the one I was to get. I looked at the cross street. I was on the corner of Flushing and Cyprus. This was the right place. The company does not have a lot or a garage. The trucks are just parked on a street in a section of Brooklyn that allows overnight parking. A section like Flushing and Cyprus.

One of the many problems with parking 15 trucks out in the open overnight is theft. Last week, one of the trucks I was driving sounded like a tank. The sound coming from underneath the truck was astounding. I pulled over and stopped the truck. I bent over and looked at the truck's undercarriage. There was a massive hole where the catalytic converter should be. Well, that was a bummer. I would have to tell someone about that at the end of the day. I didn't want to cut into my day by taking it to the shop right then. With the value of precious metals going up, catalytic converters are an easy target. They are valuable and have no identifying marks or serial numbers and can be stolen in under three minutes.

I'm standing at the truck with the wrong front license plate considering what to do next. The rain is pelting down on me. I am wearing a black slicker, but my shoes and shorts are already soaked through. The other guy to work with me today stumbles up.

"Sorry I'm late," he mumbles.

"That's ok. PJ texted me that he was going to be 15 minutes late also," I reply. The irony of someone being consistently late to a start time that they themselves have set is very, very frustrating.

I call Justin, the guy in charge of the trucks. He is the designated truck guy, but his knowledge of trucks is mostly limited to their color, if they are gas or diesel, and if the radio works. All the same, he is in charge of the trucks.

"Hey, I'm at a truck but I think it's the wrong one. The license is AA99759. I'm looking for K91845," I tell him.

"Did you look at the rear plate?" he replies with a question.

"Huh?"

"Look at the rear plate," he confirms, like that is the most obvious suggestion ever.
I walk to the back of the truck. It's K91845. I walk around to the front. Two different license plates.

"Why are the plates different?" I ask Justin.

"It's a long story," is all he says. "I have to go. Let's talk later," and with that he hangs up.

I shake my head, why would different license plates be a problem? I suppose I should just be thankful if this one has a catalytic converter. I start to go through my massive key ring. When I started driving with the company, I was given a key ring with 12 truck keys on it. I look like a school janitor who got lost on the way to work. The locks on some of these trucks don't work properly; you have to try the key on the passenger's side door as well as the driver's side door. This is possibly the worst truck in the fleet, perhaps the worst in all of Brooklyn. Sure enough, key number seven opened the truck.

Jump to five hours later. I am bleeding in the gutter with the correct license plate now staring me in the face. I see a massive hand reach down to help me up. It has to be Dylan.

Dylan is an enormous man. He is 6'6" with huge shoulders and overwhelming athleticism. He looks like the power forward on a division one basketball team, but ironically, he hates basketball.

I know this because he told me, "I hate basketball," within a few moments of meeting him.

He helps me to my feet and I stand hunched over leaning on the truck in the rain. He is standing directly over me staring at the crown of my head.

"How old are you?" he asks me. Always a weird question.

"I'm 46," I am confused by the question, but I tell him the truth. In entertainment, we are told to never say our real age. Although I think it's worse to tell someone you're 25 when you're 45 and everyone just thinks, "Man, that is the worse looking 25- year- old I have ever seen!"

"Unbelievable, you have great hair," he tells me as he looks down at my mop from above.

Dylan is 28 and yes, a good-looking physical specimen but he is very obviously losing his hair. The only people that tell me I have great hair are the people losing their hair. No one else cares, hair is something you appreciate once it's gone. You appreciate your strong legs when you have fallen off a truck and twisted your knees. It is only when we lose something that we value it.

I got COVID in March 2020 and completely lost hearing in my right ear. Apparently, the virus got into the cochlea (past my inner ear). My body beat the virus but in the process the cochlea became inflamed. The inflammation crowds out the nerve in your ear, destroying your hearing. And once the nerve degenerates there is nothing doctors can do. After seeing several specialists, it became clear I would never hear out of my right ear again. A hearing aid would not help. Hearing aids amplify the sound so the ear will pick it up. There is nothing to amplify. I have zero percent hearing. The only option is a cochlear implant which means that I would have a piece of metal protruding from the base of my skull directly behind my ear. Call me old-fashioned, but that option does not hold much appeal to me. I am not prepared to be a cyborg at the age of 46.

Losing my hearing required five trips to the doctor, minus $1,200 from JJ's car fund.

It is a very frustrating situation. I have to ask friends and strangers to repeat things again and again. And the prospect of this being the rest of my life bums me out. That being said, I never really appreciated my hearing. It was not something I even considered. It, like a lot of things, is something I took for granted. Something that I thought would always be there. Then one day, suddenly, it was not.

There are things you think you will always have in your life, but you will not. The people you believe you will always have with you will not always be there. Some will move on. Some will die. Some will abandon you, sometimes for good reason and sometimes for frivolities. But you will move on. You will continue. Long after you think you can't continue. Long after you think you are done--life will go on. Long after you lose your hearing. Or your sight. Or your legs. Or your husband. Or your house. You will go on. You will push forward.

Are you hurt or are you injured? You will get up. You are merely hurt, but it's not permanent. You will vanquish your detractors another day. Even your very survival is a testament to your strength and your ability to endure. You can do it! Live and Love. Onward.

Road Trip

"You want to pick up a truck? You'd be doing me a huge favor. I want to see my son's soccer game tonight, but we need the truck for a 7 a.m. job," is what the text from Justin read. Justin is always a little over committed, trying to do too much. He is a single dad and in over his head with work and family life.

He received a settlement of a brownstone from his divorce, but he can't afford the mortgage payments, so he had to rent it out. That story sums up his life perfectly, one step forward, two steps back.

It started as such a simple request. Pick up a truck? Sure. Where was it, the gas station?

"Nah, it's parked at the mechanic's that fixed it," he replied. Ok, no problem. Where is that?

"It's in Connecticut." That's fine. The tri-state area is where the three states meet: New Jersey, New York, and Connecticut. Depending on the time of day and amount of traffic, sometimes going to New Jersey is faster than getting to certain parts of Queens. Manhattan is separated from Queens by the East River. You could literally swim from Manhattan to Queens if you don't mind the pollution. While Jersey is viewed by some as a thousand miles from cool, it's just a stone's throw away either through a tunnel or over a hundred-year-old bridge.

Ok, no problem I think to myself and say, "I have a show at 7 p.m. but I can go after."

"Ok great. It's in Middleton, Connecticut," he tells me.

Wait, where is that? I open Google Maps; turns out Middleton is in the middle of Connecticut. Oh no, this could be a mistake.

Justin pours on the guilt now, "Yeah great, my son will be happy. I looked it up. You can take the metro north train; there is a 10 p.m. train. It's a beautiful ride, man."

Beautiful? Maybe, but after 10 p.m. it will be dark. It will be a beautiful ride with pitch black views.

"Bring a good book."

I got suckered into this one, but there's nothing I can do now.

Because of the pandemic the comedy clubs are closed, but there are a few outdoor stand-up shows in New York City during the crisis. They are a poor substitute for real stand-up. Comedians are often described as being addicted to comedy. If that is true, then stand-up is heroin, incredibly addicting and difficult to shake. If real indoor stand-up is heroin with a stage, lights, and a microphone in the house, then these outdoor shows are methadone. A poor substitute. Sure, the comedy junkies like myself chase after it, but we all know it's not the real thing. At any point, a mom in a stroller will walk right through the middle or a dog will try to urinate on your leg mid-show, both of which have happened to me.

At one show I saw, the comedian "on stage" was really struggling. A homeless person was within earshot and heard a joke. The joke did not do well. And the homeless person yelled out, "You ain't funny," which got the biggest laugh of the set. He then proceeded to play music on a Bluetooth speaker that overpowered the mic-less show and basically ended that comedian's set. He literally got played off like a modern-day gong show.

After I talk to Justin, I shower and get ready to leave the house for the show. I rent a Citi Bike, which are set up all over the city. I had looked for an electric bike and there was one left according to the app, a block from my house. When I arrive at the rack, I see a kid sitting on it waiting to take off. It's taken; I missed it by a second. Instead, I rent a regular bike. The Citi Bikes are very convenient. The only drawback is they are heavy, very heavy. It is as if someone took a Walmart Huffy bicycle that is already hefty and burdensome and added 20 pounds of steel to the frame. It's like riding a bike with your brother sitting on the handlebars, it's work.

It's August in New York and it is 82 degrees which can be nice in a desert climate, but here it holds the usual weighted-air common on the east coast in August. The moisture is thick, stuffy and suffocating.

I am sweating after riding two blocks and remind myself there are only two more miles to go. I take off my shirt and stick it in my bag. Since I am going to the train station directly after the show, I packed a bag with a change of clothes. The show is in Astoria, so I ride up from Greenpoint, swing north on McGuinness and peddle over the Pulaski Bridge.

I wore pants today, which was a mistake. I don't like to perform in shorts, but these pants make my bottom-half feel like I'm in a sauna. Given the heavy August air and my unintentional Citi Bike workout, I arrive at the show drenched. Sweat is running down my back creating a humiliating wet "belt" at the top of my pants. Additionally, there is now the outline of my wet underwear showing through by pants. This is the way I always thought my career would go.

The crowd-although I am not sure there are enough of them to be considered a crowd-has the energy of a bus stop. They are socially distanced and mostly masked, so the laughs are hard to hear. I perform while feeling like a wet puppet, then ready myself for the bike ride back down to the train. The bike takes me to the subway, which takes me to Grand Central.

Grand Central is wondrous at all times, but emptied of its people as it is presently, one feels like royalty to even walk through it.

The painted constellations on the ceiling are breathtaking, but I can't help but always notice a few minor issues. Interestingly, the painter drew a couple constellations that are no longer in use, like Musca Borealis (which is now part of Aries). What I find more troublesome is that the sky is painted backwards. The western stars are in the east and vice versa, and to add even more confusion, Orion is reversed to its original position. Why? No one knows for sure, but a guess might be that Orion was reversed so it could still face Taurus as it should. Still that means that only Orion is painted correctly.

Even more surprising is that what is painted across the ceiling scene is not the original painting. In June of 1945 as World War II dragged on, Grand Central began work to repair the ceiling which had fallen into disrepair. But inexplicably, none of the mistakes were corrected with the repairs, despite the fact Grand Central had a marketing campaign instructing school children to come learn astronomy from the painting. The ceiling is stunning, even if it is considered as a work of inverted nonfiction.

I board the train ten minutes early just to enjoy the air conditioning and the train pulls out on time. I settle down with an audio book. Tobias Wolff will get my full attention for the next two hours. Things start smoothly, the pitch-black night flying by with Mr. Wolff describing his complicated childhood in exquisite detail until the conductor comes around checking tickets.

"Train to Waterbury, right?" I confirm, handing him my ticket.

"Technically yes, but there is a problem at the station. You're going to have to get off at Bridgeport and take a bus the rest of the way," he tells me like it was the most normal thing in the world.

"A bus? Are you being serious?" I ask. I don't want to take the bus. If I wanted to take the bus, I would have bought a bus ticket.

"Yeah, it happens sometimes." Yeah, so do tsunamis but that doesn't make them fun.

Sure enough, at Bridgeport there are buses waiting for us. A local and an express. The bus is big and thankfully has a toilet on board. It also has bright green lighting lining the floors giving it an eerie look of a party bus gone wrong. The smell of weed permeates from the rear of the bus, but we all pretend not to smell it as the bus rambles on through the night. We are traveling north now, and the minutes tick by quietly.

The bus finally pulls into the station at around 1:20 a.m. It's raining. Just what I need. Me and the seven other unlucky souls pile out of the Green Lantern-like party bus. There's a man waiting by his car smoking a cigarette and looking over at us. This guy is an unusual character.

"You need a ride," he calls out.

"I'm going to Middletown, how much is that?" I ask as I walk over to get a better look at him. His teeth are small with gaps between all of them and his hair is pushed down against his skull. His clothes look oversized and there is a nervous energy about him. He acts like an alien who wants to behave as a human, but clearly hasn't figured it out yet. He gave me the willies.

"How much do you want to pay?" he asks. I realize a cab driver letting the passenger select the fare price like a game on the Price is Right is not a good sign.

"I don't know, 30 bucks?" It is 22 miles on the map. A fair offer.

"Ok, get in the car, I'll finish this cigarette," he said in no particular hurry at 1:30 a.m. As I look at the car, I get the feeling that if I get into that car, it will be the last time anyone hears from me.

I weigh the options. "Never mind," I tell him, and walk back to the relative safety of the bus stop. The bus stop has no overhang to block the rain, but sitting directly in the rain seems like a better option than going on a joy ride with this Jeffrey Dahmer.

The bus pulls out and soon it is just me and him. He's sitting on the hood of his car smoking in the rain staring at me. I decide that if he tries to make me go with him at gun point, I will just let him shoot me instead. I will not go to a second location. He will have to shoot me here.

I call an Uber. It is 15 minutes away. I only have to survive 15 minutes. The Uber is actually a Lyft and the Lyft is driven by Karen. Karen greets me loudly when she pulls up. "Kirk?" she asked, the strange man still eyeing me.

"Yep," I reply and jump in the car relieved.

"My name is Karen, but I am not a 'Karen'," she says, referencing a nickname given to certain white women in this special moment in time. I can't see her face as she is wearing a mask, but she is African American. She has a head-wrap covering her hair and is wearing a t-shirt.

As we drive off, I see the man with the little teeth climb into his car and flick his cigarette.

Karen is driving a 2015 Toyota Camry with every dash light possible on: the engine light, the brake light, ABS, maintenance required, tire pressure, airbag and fuel light are all on. It seems like a minor miracle that this car is running at all.

"Can I get gas?" Karen asks with embarrassment in her voice.

Driving for Lyft is a rough job, I've done it before. I am exhausted and my day is dragging on and on, but I feel for her. She told me this is her second job and she is just barely holding on.

"Of course, do what you have to do," I say trying to sound as cheerful as I can despite it now being almost 2:00 a.m.

"Great, I'm so sorry but we are on 'empty' and I don't know what else to do. I need gas."

"Let's get gas," I confirm. "It's all good. As long as we don't crash, you get five stars," I joke, trying to alleviate any anxious doubt she has.

These service jobs where the public gives ratings on the service are a nightmare for the workers. For their very jobs to be in jeopardy by a passenger who may very well be drunk, or worse, seems grossly unfair. I go inside to get an iced tea for my long drive ahead while Karen gets gas. When I return with my tea in hand, I see she has pumped eight dollars exactly.

Off we go.

We talk about Connecticut. She talks about a recent racist issue that has happened to her and that she misses the Bronx but there is more work in Connecticut. She tells me what her life is like here and then the conversation turns to her family.

"Yeah, my kids are getting big. The youngest is 11. She is a handful. She is so stubborn, I don't know what I'm going to do with her. She don't listen. I told her…," her phone rings interrupting her.

"I'm so sorry, let me just get this, it's my boyfriend," the phone has rung three times in the 15 minutes I have been in the car.

"I told you, I'm driving, I can't talk right now," she says in a tone much sharper than she has been talking to me. We can only talk with that level of distain to someone we love. It's probably not healthy, but it's normal.

"Ok, ok, I'm just calling to check on you. Call me back," he says gruffly but apologetically. The call is routed through the bluetooth and speaker and I can hear the concern in his voice and he seems relieved that she has answered.

"He calls me all the time," she says. Her words and face express annoyance but her tone sounds like she appreciates the attention. "He just can't get enough of me; he calls all the time," she says with a slight grin.

After the call, she continues to talk about her kids and her concerns if they don't open the schools.

We finally arrive at the truck dealership. The truck is there like he said. I knew it was the right truck, our truck, cause it is the only one covered in spray can doodles. That tacky yet delightful art on our trucks that I recognize immediately. The door is unlocked and the keys in the visor.

I tip Karen on the app. As a rule, I like to tip 20%, but I should have tipped her more and in cash; she needed it. But I didn't, and I regret it. By the time I arrive at the lot, it is after 2:00 a.m. and I'm exhausted. Now I'm thinking about the truck and hope it will start. I'm in my own head, consumed with my own problems. After saying goodbye, Karen drives off to see her kids and her concerned boyfriend and to sleep a few hours before she has to wake up and do it all again tomorrow.

And I will get into a 28-foot Hino truck and drive the 100 miles back to Brooklyn. Back over the Whitestone Bridge. Down the expressway, back down, deep into Brooklyn to side streets with lax parking rules where I will park it after 4:00 a.m. and give the truck a few hours to rest too. Then it will be picked up later by other working men with families who are trying to get that bread to pay down bills, to put gas in their cars, eight dollars at time, to push back the debt collectors and eviction notices. The truck will be driven around, filled and emptied many times today with someone's treasures. It will be used as a tool to make this little world go around, one more day at a time so Karens and Justins can spend another day with their children, watch baseball game and take calls from their loved ones. Progress. Slow but steady progress.

Big Sean

Although Andy had talked to me about this job several years ago, it wasn't until several months ago that I reached out and confirmed I wanted to pursue it. Little did I know it would be most of my summer. They say money does not buy happiness, (but it does buy you pizza). I knew the job would require physical labor, but what I didn't realize was it would expose me to an eclectic assortment of interesting characters that I never would have crossed paths with normally. This job has taught me several things, including how to properly wrap a couch. But more importantly, I've realized we are all very different, each peculiar in our own little ways. Making human connections is hard enough, but add in the trauma of the world coming to a stand-still and it can seem nearly impossible. Sometimes the goal is just to understand someone different from you, get along as gracefully as possible, and move on to the next day with more patience than you had the day before.

Let me explain. Some people love the mornings. I am not one of those people. My brain really starts humming around 6 p.m. which is a real shame for anyone who has to deal with me at an earlier hour.

People who have had to see me within an hour of my waking know the unintentional menace of my attitude at that time. Parents, siblings, roommates, and anyone else who has had the displeasure of waking me up, know my glowering mug upon being awakened. Even flight attendants who have gently tried to waken me to straighten my seat before landing have seen my cantankerous nature. I hate breaking the peaceful slumber. Even if I am having bad dreams, the real nightmare is waking up.

Today is Thursday. I wake up to a text at 6 a.m. It's from PJ. "Hey, can you pick me up at the entrance of Canal Street?"

It's moving day. Again. As it has been for the last few months.

I am the driver, but the crew and I are supposed to meet at the truck and then drive together to the job. However, sometimes someone (like PJ) will want me to pick them up en route to the job. If the pick-up is on the way, that is to say, if it does not add any additional time to the trip, I am fine with it. It shortens their day which they like, I understand that. It's when it makes my start time even earlier than it has to be that I get a little prickly. You want to get picked up cause it saves you an hour. Listen, I get it, I'm just not interested in running an Uber service in a 30-foot box truck through downtown Manhattan. Let's meet somewhere on the way.

Today I work with PJ, who is a morning person and often texts me before I get up. Every time it's something different with him, but he is consistent in frustrating me. I pick him up where he asked me to, saving him an hour of his day. This time, he gets into the truck cab with a canned nitrogen coffee and for some reason he shakes it. As he pulls at the tab, I start to yell, already seeing what is going to happen.

"No. No. No." But it's too late. As he opens it the can predictably explodes all over the cab and all over both us.

"I guess I shouldn't have shaken that," explains Captain Obvious with a pained look on his face.

You think, you boob? I was so mad it made me laugh like a lunatic. Seems counter intuitive, but I was just in shock at the stupidity. I start the day off covered in sticky coffee and milk on a day that will be over 100 degrees. There's nothing like starting a day of strenuous physical labor covered in a bath of dairy, so I can smell like sour, spoiled milk all day.

I am enjoying this job even during this crazy time. Maybe it is the cash at the end of the job that forces a strong correlation between work and survival. I know from experience that office jobs offer the opposite. There is something disconnecting and banal about getting up for a job, working for weeks, and then seeing a number on a bank account app on your phone indicating that money has been deposited. I suppose I am not evolved enough to get the connection. In contrast, "Hey, move that from here to there, and also take these crisp hundreds," is very easy for my primal brain to understand. "Kirk strong. Kirk move box to there. Then Kirk get cookie."

It's August and we are at the end of the month, which is creatively called The Rush. There are thousands of people who want to move in August and most moves are concentrated around the beginning and ending of the month. I am told that the last week of July and first week of August are always a mess. Crews are asked to work 12-14 hour days, just grinding away at helping people chase their dreams in new homes. When the company runs out of trucks, they rent trucks. If you are new or unlucky (read me) you are assigned a rental truck. While the rental trucks are usually nicer than the company trucks, they have to be picked up at the rental office, which adds at least another 45 minutes of driving to your day.

There is very little traffic at 6:00 a.m. and I arrive at CC rentals in Long Island City, Queens at 6:45. There are 15 people lingering at the checkout booth in line in front of me. I recognize half a dozen of them.

I see Stalkie in line. Stalkie is his actual legal name, not a nickname from a traumatized ex. He once stopped in the middle of traffic and got out of his truck to confront another driver over a driving altercation. He won the fight, but lost the war, once the cops were called and they were both arrested. It's hard to be paid for delivery when you're cooling your heels in jail from trying to full body suplex someone.

Also in line I see Bengay. Yes, his name is just like the cooling ointment. The name is unusual and confusing, just like him. He is overly athletic, has a huge Cheshire grin, and is prone to telling terrible jokes. "Your wife died huh, are you rich now?" he asked me within 10 minutes of meeting me the first time.

"If I was rich would I be moving couches? That's not how that works," I explained. "But who knows, maybe you'll be able to find out someday," I reply with a weary grin and immediately wish I could take it back. He smiled. I could see the little wheels in his head turn and his eyes go up and to the right, and then the smile slowly fade. Sometimes, my tongue gets the best of me and I say something honest, but also mean. While it might be true, my saying it was unnecessary and cutting.

Looking around the rest of the scattered crowd, I see Shane. Shane is small, 5′5″ 140 pounds, but very strong. If you can be a mover at this size, you have to be strong like a little ant who can carry 10 times its own weight. His teeth are spaced apart in a haphazard manner. He chain smokes and always looks nervously at the floor, eyes shifting around as if he is looking for lost coins when he talks.

There is a story about him that I heard the first day I worked at the company. He was working with Hughes who is a much bigger man. They get cut off in traffic. An argument ensues with another driver. The driver slams on his brakes in front of the moving truck. Hughes who is driving the moving truck starts to get out and looks over at Shane in the passenger seat. Before Hughes can get his belt off Shane is already out the truck and has pulled a knife out of his pocket.

"So it's like that?" Hughes says.

They get out of the truck. The other driver sees there are two of them and one of him. And the little one who looks like a carny has a knife. The other driver wisely gets back in his car and finishes his day without being stabbed.

Seeing Shane here standing in line looking very meek, his story is hard to believe. I nod at Shane, "So, you stab anyone today yet?" I ask him smiling.

He looks sheepishly at the ground. "No. But I've been here an hour," he says.

Oh no, this is not a good sign. It should take just minutes to check out the truck. The moving company rents a dozen or so around this time every month.

“I guess the boss’s credit card has been turned down,” he fills me in. Alex is the owner of the company and is as disorganized as you might expect from someone who runs a moving business in Brooklyn that only takes cash. Yep, it's a cash business. How does that work you might ask? I have no idea, but it does and has for years.

After waiting for 30 minutes, I’m asked if I want to use my credit card to reserve the truck; I laugh heartedly and shake my head no, then I reconsider. I am a miles junkie and I could use the credit card accrued miles toward one of my trips to see my son. Who cares if I earn the miles on one of these crazy moves, this cavalcade of sweat and Ikea beds that don't travel well. After all, miles are miles, regardless of how they are accrued, I plunk down my card.

It’s now 7 a.m., the sun has already risen in the east showering Manhattan with its golden rays. There are fewer people than normal out. It’s in the low 70s, a red herring if there ever was one, as this day is to be in the mid 90s later with smothering humidity that will push everyone who can be indoors.

There is a simple dignity to being essentially a laborer, if not an essential worker. These guys are all out here, not for the love of moving boxes, but to get their money, for themselves and their families. There is no pretension of grandeur of what is going on here. They came to work. To move a few thousand pounds of furniture and boxes with their bodies. Down staircases or elevators, on to trucks, to be driven through crowded streets and then to houses, garages, or sometimes back up different staircases into very similar apartments.

We arrive at the job and there is a parking spot that would fit a sedan. The client has been holding the spot for us, which is a very nice gesture.

“Let me move my car, here is a spot. Will this truck fit there?” the client asks.

"Oh, sure it will," says PJ before I get a word out. PJ is in his late twenties, thin, about 6 foot and known to always wear colorful hats. He is indecisive and gets flustered when others are waiting for him to make decisions, which can be frustrating. PJ has been appointed as the "point" crew leader today. He has been promoted to point and then promptly demoted twice, only be be promoted once again. This has rattled his confidence which has only added to his own second guessing. That makes him extra sensitive. I asked him earlier if there was something I could do to help and he stated that I should "focus on the driving and I'll focus on the pointing," which didn't exactly sit great with me considering I still smelled like sour milk from his exploding coffee. A younger me might have stopped the truck and had a heart to heart with him, but this new older me knows there is no point.

He jumps out of the truck with the idea of helping me to back up. The problem is he doesn't drive so his directions into a parallel parking spot are not terrific. He waves the truck back but has already backed me into a tree branch on an earlier job. My slow pace when reversing was the only thing that saved the truck from extensive damage that time.

"Yo, that's a tree branch you backed me into," I say, sounding like a truck driver from the 70s.

"Hey, my bad, man," he says repeating the same phrase he said when he sprayed me with the coffee. He says it with a slight accent which sounds more Georgia than Florida where he is actually from. He says it so much at this point it's becoming a catchphrase, sounds like Urkel's "Did I do that?" All he needs now is the suspenders. He already has the glasses and frame.

We get through the day without damaging the truck or having any more drinks explode. Considering today's crew, that's a win. Sometimes it's a war of attrition and I just try to limit my losses. Tomorrow is a new day.

The next day is Friday. I am working with Hughes. I have only worked with him a few times before. There is something very weird about working with someone wearing a mask all day. I have worked several 14-hour days with him and seen his face for only a few seconds. I do remember he has a protruding jaw, he's 6'2," and very solidly built. He likes to wear skater shoes and long So Cal style cargo shorts that can be called capris.

I ask him what got him into this line of business.

"I was a professional skater, been all over the world," he says. That explains the shorts and shoes. I didn't even really know that skating was a real job, but I guess if you can make a living playing video games about skateboarding, you should be able to make a living skateboarding. I did notice that he has those fat ankles that look like they have been rolled again and again.

Today we are working with a third man. Carlos, the guy who makes the schedule, had called me the day before and told me a new guy was starting tomorrow and we would be the first job he works on.

"You're going to love this guy," Carlos gushes. He's so excited about him, as if he's a matchmaker or a shadkhan determined to find me my soulmate.

"His name is Big Sean, you're going to love this guy." Carlos repeats. "Ok", I say plainly." It's not like he's really asking my opinion. It's Rush Season. There are too many moves and Carlos is clearly desperate for workers.

Well, Big Sean arrives and he is big. But this job is not modeling, where you just stand around with a pretty face. Here, you have to move and lift things. Also, he's 30 minutes late, which is not my favorite thing as it means we are now all late. At this job we are splitting the money in equal parts. So, if you're not pulling your weight and we're all getting paid the same amount at the end of the day, it's easy to get frustrated.

"I got lost," he says while holding a Dunks iced coffee, pausing and looking as if he is expecting a reaction. Did you get lost in a Dunks? Also NYC is famously laid out on a grid system. Streets start with 1st Street in the south part of Manhattan and continue up numerically into the 200s as you head north ending in the Bronx. Horizontal avenues across the city start with 1st Ave in the east and progress to 11th in the west. If you are from NYC, it is not hard to know where you are if you are on a corner with two numbers. If you're from NYC and you can't find 33rd Street and 7th Ave, you are not trying. And while we are at it, if you stop for coffee while running late, have the decency to throw away the evidence before arriving. If you arrive late holding a fancy drink and everyone else on the team is covered in sweat carrying boxes, your coworkers might feel the inequality of the arrangement.

Big Sean joins Hughes and me already packing the truck. After his first trip up the stairs he says, "This is hard."

"Yeah man, how did you think we were getting this furniture down, with a forklift?" Hughes says. Hughes has zero patience. This is his 5th season with the company, and he sees people come and go.

"I'm getting cramps," Big Sean says.

I nod trying to look understanding even though he's almost 20 years younger than me.
"Ok," I say and weakly smile as I head back up the stairs to get more boxes. I come back down and he is still leaning on the truck. This is not good; we could really use his help. This is a big job and I try to encourage him.

"Come on buddy, let's just get a couple boxes."

He silently starts to walk with me as if I am leading him to the electric chair. I feel bad. It's like the scene in the movie the Green Mile. I am the Tom Hanks character, the likable idiot and he is the giant with a good heart. As we walk towards the building, I half expect someone to yell out, "Dead man walking."

We pick up a couple of boxes and head back down the stairs. When we get to the truck, he puts the boxes on the truck and sits on the back of the truck.

"Catch your breath and come back up in a minute," I tell him, trying to sound encouraging.

I emerge from the building again and see him still on the truck, but now his shoes and socks are off and he's rubbing his bare feet. It is quite a sight and it looks a little like a bear checking between his toes. At this point, I don't know what else to do. I put the boxes on the truck and go back up for more. When I emerge this time, I don't see him at all. I check the cab, but he's nowhere to be seen. Was he not real? Did I imagine the whole thing? Was Big Sean just a Big apparition? I don't have time to look for him. The sun is already beating down and losing a man is going to significantly add more work to the already large job. On my next trip up to get boxes, I tell Hughes who has been in the apartment wrapping furniture what is going on.

"I don't know man, he's gone," I say and can't help but laugh a little, which confuses Hughes who is very serious.

"I don't get it. What's the joke? Why is it funny?" he replies while still wrapping cling wrap around a couch.

"No joke man, he's gone. One minute he's on the truck barefoot, rubbing his naked feet. Next minute he's gone," I say laughing again. "It's not funny, it's just weird I guess," I say unconvincingly.

"Unbelievable man, Carlos always gives me the new guys." Hughes has his mask on, so I can't see if he's smiling, but he doesn't sound amused.

I don't know what happened to my man Big Sean. In my mind, he got on the subway wearing his mask, but no shoes. Sitting down. Just rubbing his feet like a freshly released circus bear. Free, but unsure of what was next for him. He rumbled back to his apartment where there are no boxes to carry.

This job is not for everyone and there is nothing wrong with that, you got your feet wet and it's not for you. It takes time to find a job that you can embrace. Don't give up, keep looking. Some day you'll find your feet, maybe as a foot masseuse or maybe at foot locker. Until that day don't get discouraged, keep moving forward one lumbering step at a time.

It was nice to meet you Big Sean, good luck on all your foot adventures.

Fight Island

Today we are moving a lady from 152 2nd Ave. to Hoboken, New Jersey and I am working with Santos and Xavier. Usually workers don't just wander off but it turns out it is the same Santos that had walked off the job we had been working on together previously, not that I recognized him. Early in the summer Santos and I were assigned to the same crew. Santos looks like a retired college running back. Stout with powerful legs and arms, at least they looked powerful. He looked like he could do the job, but when tested under fire he had come up short, he quit an hour into the second job of the day. The last thing he said to me was " I got cramps man, I got to go" and I thought I would never see him again.

It had been a busy summer and when I got the truck at 8 a.m., I could not place his face.

"Hey, Santos. Nice to meet you man," I offer up trying to be as friendly as possible to the new face.

"I've worked with you before," he tells me.

I could not recall his face at all but tried to be cordial. "Oh cool, good to see you again," which is what I always say when I can't remember someone.

"Yeah, we did a job together, but I got cramps and had to go home," he continues.

"Ohhh yeah," I say, more excitedly than I meant to sound. "I remember you! I thought you quit?" I was excited to be able to recall him, not the fact that he had left me to move furniture by myself, but my overt enthusiasm seemed misplaced when discussing someone's failure.

"I didn't quit," he says sounding a little hurt. "I had just worked a lot that day and got cramps, I had to go home."

That is the definition of quitting, I thought, but I didn't say that— I didn't want to be a jerk. I immediately switched gears and said meekly, "Oh right, of course."

This is a big job today- it's hot, and we definitely need him. Doing a three-man job with two men is rough. It will take longer, affecting the tip. You better not quit, you quitter, is what I thought, but I said nothing.

I get the dollies out of the truck to begin the load. He continues with the details of the day he had cramps and I do my best to pretend to listen to this deserter who'd left us a man short in the summer heat.

Xavier jumped in cutting him off, "You'll be fine today, just do your best."

Xavier is an actor. He grew up in San Diego, the son of a military man. He is 6'4", very strong, and sports a very full and well-defined afro. Another interesting fact about Xavier is that he can fall asleep mid conversation in a moving truck.

"There is something about the movement of the truck that knocks me out," he explained to me once. "When I was a baby, if I couldn't sleep my parents used to drive me around until I fell asleep. Now the only problem is at night in my bed, I can't sleep a wink."

The last time I worked with him we were assigned a move that was going to the south Jersey coast. After loading the truck, we began the two-hour drive to deliver the items. To pass the time we were listening to AM sports radio.

The tinny speakers of this Hino truck belting out a static-filled announcer's voice, "That's it for the pre-game. Coming up next Notre Dame vs Pittsburg. Fighting Irish ranked 4th in the nation, undefeated, should be a tough game for Pitt."

Xavier jumped in, "Can't wait to hear this game, Notre Dame should win the ACC for sure this year."

At the first drive of the game the play call came in on the radio, "Quarterback Ian Book throws down the middle and caught! It's Ben Skowronek with his first touchdown as a member of the Notre Dame Fighting Irish."

"Hey," I said excitedly to Xavier "correct call" and looked over at him. He was already asleep.

But today he is wide awake as we load the truck while trying to keep one eye on meter maids and another eye on the weather. The forecast is for a little rain which would make everything much slower and slicker, but today we get lucky. We finish the load and pull down the back gate and place a small lock on it.

We start the short journey through the city out of the Holland Tunnel and on to Jersey. Xavier passes in and out of sleep. He falls asleep, we hit a bump, his head hits the window hard, and he is back in the land of the living for a few minutes, until being jostled back to sleep. Santos is on his phone looking at pretty girls on Instagram who will never reply to his DM's. I tune the radio to 1050 AM, ESPN's affiliate in NYC.

The talking heads are discussing the upcoming MMA fight. It is Khabib Nurmagomedov vs Justin Gaethje fighting for the 155 lb. championship. The fight is to take place on Fight Island. Fight Island is on an actual island in the Emirates. In a strange twist, during this unique time period, prize fights are taking place on an island, in front of no fans. If you describe what is happening it sounds like a dystopian future. Poor fighters from impoverished third world countries or poor domestic counties are flown into the rich oil kingdoms of the Middle East, stripped down to their underwear and made to fight for money. The fights are filmed and shown all over the world to huddled unemployed masses staying home, waiting out a virus that threatens to kill indiscriminately. If this story line was pitched as a major movie plot it might be thought too bleak, yet here we are. These are the lives we are living.

The commentators on the radio are taking calls from listeners giving their thoughts on who will win the upcoming fight. The host of the show speaks with that radio voice rhythm (i.e. fake energy) customary in his field.

"We have Chris calling in from India…India? Sorry, Indiana, that makes more sense. Who do you got tonight, Chris?" he almost sang into the mic.

The caller responds in a very nasally voice, "I got Justin. He's going to knock Khabib out. He might decapitate him."

"Wow," the host responds. "Everyone is picking the underdog today. What is happening? Do you guys know something we don't?"

Xavier, who I didn't even realize was awake, chimed in. "Nah, that guy lives in his mom's basement. He knows nothing. Khabib's takedowns are insane, he's putting him out. Justin is going to be sleeping like a baby in his arms."

The hosts of the show go back and forth a little discussing the fight and one says, "I don't know, Justin has been working hard. His boxing is coming around. If he keeps it upright, he's got a shot."

I turn to Xavier, "What do you think of his boxing?" But it was too late, he was out like a light. In what could not have been more than two minutes, Xavier is already asleep. Earlier he had been complaining about neck pain and now I know why. As he sleeps his head bounces around atop of his body. Bobbing this way and that, east to west and north to south—like a giant bobble head nodding at me all the way down the New Jersey coast.

The route we are taking is scenic. New Jersey, like all of us, is a paradox. There are industrial parts with aging refineries that are the antithesis of picturesque. They present an industrial decay that wouldn't be out of place in the Eastern European Soviet Bloc. Yet, just a few miles from these places are green forests and gorgeous landscapes, the kind that have inspired artists for generations. This forest we are driving by has a lake in it and it reminds me a little of Sweden. It may have been because I just returned from visiting my son, JJ and it has been at the forefront of my mind.

While some of the scenery looks similar to Sweden, culturally Sweden does its own thing. It's the land of milk and honey, if the milk is made of Filmjölk, and the honey into Swedish fish. Filmjölk is a Nordic delicacy made of fermented milk that tastes as good as it sounds. The dairy goes down as easily as the word flows off your tongue. I'm told it's an acquired taste, which is what everyone says about things that taste bad, like beer, cigarettes and durian---that "amazing" fruit that actually smells like stinky feet.

My son has two passports, one Swedish, his sole inheritance from his recently departed mother. He lives in Sweden as the care he gets there is excellent and at this point in my life, it's what I can afford—free. If life smiled on me and things turned around, I would love to have him live closer. Currently, it is our best option and one that I'm constantly thankful for. Sweden has chosen to fully fund programs for the disabled, and that is something that while probably not on most people's short list of important things for a society, is at the top of mine for obvious reasons.

Disability is a challenging thing. At age two, it was very apparent to me that my son was disabled. There are things that my son did at three, like run around naked, that were cute considering his size and appearance, but became less "cute" as he became a man. Running naked through a store. Cute at three. Unsettling at 23. Stealing French fries off someone's table at a McDonald's. Cute at three. Theft at 23. Being overtly interested in and grabbing women's boobs cute at three, assault at 23.

The care of a man who is 6 feet tall and 230 pounds, but who also has the mind of a child is complicated. He has always been curious, getting into whatever he saw around the house and literally looking behind the surface of things. In his last apartment before his current one, he got curious as to what was under the solid wood floorboards and ripped them up by hand.

His strength was never in doubt--he is strong. He also tore off the molding that framed the doors and windows. More than once he has ripped a door off its hinges by grabbing the top, putting his foot against it at the bottom as a counterweight and pulling. No one taught him this. He learned it himself. It makes me equal parts proud and terrified that at any moment he can create thousands of dollars of damage. Once he was was curious about the pipes that led to the bathroom sink. He grabbed one and pulled it from its housing creating a geyser which delighted him and perturbed the rest of us. He'd made his own little private water park.

When he turned 19 his mother and I made the tough decision to move him into a group home. I never second guess a family making the best decision they can for their disabled loved one. It is a tough and deeply personal decision, that each one must make with their own best judgment. Some people decide when that loved one is 7 or 14, and some never do. But for us we decided at 19 that it would be better for everyone if he lived there. The physical move was minimal. There was little to move. He consistently destroyed furniture so all of our furniture was moved only twice. Initially into our house and the second time to the curb to be picked up by the garbage man. The emotional adjustments were harder. Apparent small decisions were fraught with emotional landmines that at any time could explode into hurt feelings and tears. He didn't want to be away from his mother's side, but she couldn't physically handle him. He would from time to time physically hurt her and it made it difficult if not impossible to continue to take care of him. It took him a few weeks to adapt to his new place but once adjusted, he has never been happier. It has been a great decision for us, and especially for him.

Many people with autism have specific interests or hobbies that dominate a large part of their lives. It might be trains, flight schedules, or perhaps cars. For my JJ it is video clips, specifically video clips of cartoons and animated motion pictures. His favorites are Veggie Tales, Barney, Teletubbies, and the movie Prince of Egypt. If you let him, he will sit all day on his bed and watch videos. The same songs again and again. He will look up Prince of Egypt on YouTube and watch it in multiple languages. He is nonverbal, meaning he doesn't really communicate, so I don't know what he understands, but I know he likes the songs from that movie. He will repeat things he has heard and then look at us with raised eyes asking us with his gestures to repeat back the lines from the movies also. When we do it, he squeals with joy.

Videos used to mean VCR tapes. Our home always had several large rubber tubs full of tapes, different colors and conditions, but all important to one special boy. I don't miss the tubs and moving them around. I also don't miss being an unofficial VHS repair man tasked with pulling yards of damaged tape and a variety of food items, usually peanut butter and jelly sandwiches from the machine.

As a child he had tactile issues, meaning he could not stand the way some things felt. At the time, one of the calming solutions was to brush his legs and arms with a special soft brush. Another unofficial treatment that we implemented was roughhousing. He loved for me to wrestle with him. I would tickle and poke, pull at him and make him play. It became one of his favorite things. About halfway through play time I would lay on my back with my knees pulled up to my chest and he would lay on my legs. I would grab his hands and then I would extend my legs throwing him in the air while he shrieked with delight. I travel to see him several times a year and on this last trip, he had tried to lay on my legs, something we had not done in many years, yet clearly he remembered doing it earlier. I was able to extend my legs only once, but at such a slow pace he definitely did not fly through the air. Honestly, I was just happy to not blow out an ACL My body is more designed for nerdy desk work than powering giant men into the air with a flick of my leg, and I was lucky to do it even once unscathed. We wrestled every day I was there.

JJ has struggled with general intestinal issues for many years and physical activity would help him make sure there was a "flow". The problem is that while mostly potty trained, he still struggles with accidents, which are hard for me. I don't like cleaning up the feces of another grown man. Each of these visits to see my son occur several months apart and the time apart brings into focus the changes in him and his development. While the progress might be very gradual and slow, it is very apparent when observed at three-month intervals.

On my fifth day there (out of an 8-day trip) we took a seafront walk in the woods. I had rented a house about 25 minutes from Sundsvall, where he lives. It was on the Gulf of Bothnia technically part of the Baltic Sea, a usually serene place. Thirty minutes into the walk, JJ started to cross his legs. I knew what that meant: he had to go to the bathroom. I led him next to a tree, but he would not go. That was odd. But we continued. A few minutes later he said, "Poop in potty" which was something that we had taught him years and years ago that had stuck. He had to use a toilet. I told him excitedly, "Good talking." We turned around and headed back to the house.

We made it no more than five minutes when he had an accident. He was very upset. He looked at me with a pained expression that conveyed embarrassment and sadness. I tried my best to put on my forced smile and we soldiered back to the rental house. I recalled all the times I had gone through this before. Potty training has been a two-decades long battle for us, sometimes won and sometimes lost. Today we had lost the battle and now had to head back to camp to pick up the pieces metaphorically and literally. I showered him off and looked forward to a fresh start.

The trip made it clear to me that JJ needs a car. He may never be able to drive, but he needs wheels to get around. In addition to the toilet issues, it's hard to ride the bus with him. He doesn't always follow instructions and when he misses a bus stop it can mean a several mile walk back to where he should have gotten off. As he is hard to control, often his aides just don't take him out. But he needs to get out of the house. A car that he and the other residents of the home can use is a good solution. And with this job so far, I have saved enough for half of the car.

My mind is brought back to the present as the GPS announces we have arrived at the destination. I awaken Sleeping Beauty and Santos takes a break from sliding into DM's.

We begin to unload the truck and I am pleasantly surprised. Despite his prior history of deserting, Santos is doing well! Not great, but good enough. The client's new home is a third floor walk-up. Santos, Xavier, and I have organized this move. Each of us will move each object on to the next person. Santos brings the item from the truck to the second floor. From there, I take it to the third floor where Xavier will take it from me to its final destination. Every once in a while, Santos slows down and I walk down two flights where he is struggling and help him carry his load. But overall, he does well. And most importantly, he does not quit. He is improving, and there is less complaining.

Despite the mishaps, Santos is making progress. Similar to JJ, his improvements are in fits and starts, but there is progress nonetheless.

In the end, the last Sweden trip had been good. JJ and I experienced a couple major poop accidents, but not every day. And each accident was proceeded with him warning us ahead of time, which is both a big help and improvement from where he had started as a young boy learning how to use the bathroom.

When I feel discouraged about my progress in life, I remember regardless of how slowly I go, the advances will come if I keep moving forward. We may not always progress at the pace we want, but growth will happen if we put in the time. This is true for me, for you, for JJ, and for Santos.

We finish up and start the hour-long drive back from Jersey to the city. I think about how Santos has done. I think about JJ improving, slow, but steady progress.

I flick on the AM radio to listen to some highlights.

We hear the sports update from the sports news host. "And in sports news, Khabib has won the 155 lb. championship, rendering Justin unconscious in the third round. After the fight he placed his gloves in the center of the ring at Fight Island and announced his retirement."

I laugh. Xavier had called it. Santos would be fine. And the fight, he was right. I turn to Xavier who is sitting next to me on the bench in the truck cab to congratulate him, but he did not hear the radio. He was already asleep, head bouncing along to the bumps of the uneven road. His head unknowingly nodding to his prescient comments from earlier.

Whatever we are struggling to overcome will work itself out. But we must keep moving forward. Always forward.

Baby Steps

"Get out of the car right now, you piece of s***," Rob screamed.

Rob was standing outside of the driver's window of a BMW and yelling at the top of his lungs. His face was red. His hair was thinning and you could see the red scalp poking through the wisps of hair. Rob cut a menacing figure. He was about 5'10", powerfully built and covered in arm and leg hair. Always wanting to carry the heaviest furniture, he supplemented his daily gym trips with daily moves. He was the only mover I knew who would try to sprint up the steps every time. Every-time.

Sitting in a legally parked BMW was a terrified businessman, who refused to get out of his luxury car.

We had double parked the moving truck directly in front of the client's new apartment. We were not legally parked, but it was our only option on this packed Brooklyn neighborhood. We unloaded the truck as quickly as we could, helped by Rob trying to sprint things up the stairs. And we had nearly finished unloading when the red BMW arrived. Before it arrived, there was still room for cars to pass our double-parked truck. That ended when this man in his fancy car parked parallel to us directly across the street. Now no one could get by. We had been alerted to it by someone's blaring car horn, New York City's informal soundtrack. We had exited the apartment and Rob approached the new car.

We were moving two young men perhaps in their early 20s. They were at that age where mom was still there helping them. Mom was a woman perhaps in her late forties, but with the clothes of a much older woman. She was a kind faced lady with her hair covered up by a hat and a long dress all the way to her ankles. Her arms were also mostly covered as she walked from her minivan to the apartment carrying a care package for her son. She wore dark colors and must have been Mennonite or some other very strict religious group. She was clearly a person for whom even color is unnecessary or an ostentatious frivolity, a vanity that is to be overcome. What color is sin? Apparently anything except white or black.

"Hey, can you pull your car up about 15 feet?" Rob had said to the driver, starting the whole conversation out on a note that was not indicative as to how this would play out.

"Nah, I'm waiting for someone," the man said, while holding a cell phone in his right hand and pushing the button to roll up the window with his left hand.

"Hey, I'm asking nice, we are working here. Please move your car." Rob said with his face starting to redden.

"No bro, I don't want to," was the reply that sent Rob over the top.

"Yo! Move your car brother, or I'll move it for you." Rob was instantly red and it caught the man off guard. He stared at him wide-eyed still holding his phone, shaking his head no, and saying he did not want to.

"I'm not asking, I'm telling you. Move your car or I'm going to shove this mirror ..." Rob continued and explained that the mirror would be placed inside the man's anatomy. He then further explained the other things that would be done to him in terrifyingly accurate detail. He was gesturing wildly with his hands. Acting out the actions that his words had declared; the right hand could do this and the left hand this. His hands matched his words, showing clearly what he wanted to do and why. There was a strange, unnerving passion in his voice. It was almost as if he had been hoping this would happen; that Santa had gotten his letter and finally granted his wish.

The man pointed his camera phone at Rob and I can only assume began to record. But he refused to get out of the car. Honestly, that was the right move. Rob would have torn him limb from limb like a Raggedy Ann doll.

Rob grabbed at the door handle several times which was locked and yelled at the man only inches from the window. I was at a distance but could see the little spit projectiles exiting his mouth and making their new home on the driver's side exterior window. The man continued to record, but in a display of his intelligence, said nothing other than no, hoping to not antagonize the bear any more than he already was antagonized. Rob epitomized the phrase "stomping mad"; he literally lifted up off the ground a few times.

This happened my first week on the job and I had no idea what to make of it. The escalation from zero to 60 in seconds struck me as hilarious. Although the threat of violence seemed real, the level of anger and reaction time was cartoonish and I couldn't help but laugh. It was crazy. I knew if the man got out of his car, I would have to step in to make sure there was not a homicide, but all the same, I couldn't stop laughing. However, I tried to laugh quietly as to not anger or poke the bear and somehow become myself the target of the attention.

At this point there were eight cars waiting to get by, all honking. It was a musical cacophony of different horns, some imported cars, some domestic. Then a truck came along and blared a distinctively loud truck honk indicating play time was over and the adults were here.

Rob looked up from his tirade and saw the box truck at the end of the line behind all the cars impatiently waiting to get by.

"I'm circling the block and then I'm coming back for you. This is not over," he said pointing at the man through the glass. He pointed using his index finger, bouncing it off the side window glass so hard I wondered if anyone had ever broken shatter-resistant glass with just their index finger. The sound made against the glass was so loud, I could hear it even from my vantage point 20 feet away.

He walked to the back of the truck, reached up and grabbed the strap on the rear gate. He slammed the gate with such ferocity the box shook. For one second, I thought it might collapse like the house made of straw by a little pig. But the box held as the sound echoed off the three-story brick houses lining the street.

In an instant Rob was in the cab of the truck and the engine roared to life. The truck pulled out at such speed I was curious if he would make that first right around the block or if the truck would roll over in protest. He made the turn which was unfortunate for the man in the BMW who was still filming the whole thing on his cell phone.

I stood at the front door laughing in shock. I couldn't believe what I had witnessed. Had that actually happened?

The cars that had been held up were now flowing through at a steady clip, slowing slightly to look in at the man that they had seen get yelled at with a ferocity that is normally reserved more for someone who had just administered the wrong meds to a dying patient.

As the last car in line trickled by, I looked over to my right where I saw the client's mom still holding the food she had taken from her brown minivan. She stood with her feet glued to the ground and her mouth slightly agape in shock.

She had witnessed the whole thing.

We made eye contact and I raised my eyebrows as if to say, "Crazy, right?"

"Wow, well. He's got quite a mouth on him doesn't he," she said while shaking her head and starting into the house. I am guessing the event had exposed her to a few words she had not heard for a while, perhaps ever. I, who live in NYC, was surprised by some of the conjugations and free use of grammar. Some nouns had become verbs in Rob's rant and rave. The ferocity of actions Rob wanted to perform were outside of the normal rules of grammar and nature, I presume.

And in an instant Rob was back. The truck was parked in the same spot. He jumped out and raised the rear gate of the truck. I did my best to not smile or laugh. There was a third mover working that day, Adam. The three of us continued unloading the last few items from the truck.

Rob yelled out at his antagonist. "I'm not done with you. I have plans for you and your mirror," as he channeled his energy to run boxes up to the second-floor apartment.

In less than 10 minutes we were done. The BMW was still there and the man was still on his phone. He looked over wide eyed at Rob and tried to not look scared even though his face was betraying him.

We finished folding the blankets we had been using and closed the back. Rob stood for a second staring at the car.

"Hey bud, we have another move we have to get to," I offered. It was true and unless he was going to break the window with a rock and pull the man out of the car with his bare hands, there was nothing he could do.

"Yep, I know," he said, still looking at the car. "I have to go settle up with the client." Rob went inside and spoke with the two young men and the mother who had been outside. He then exited the building and climbed in the truck where Adam and I were already sitting.

"Ok boys, let's go." And with that we took off.

We rode in silence for about 10 minutes as Rob's face slowly returned to its natural color. He had dark hair and a thick beard. The hair on his chin being thicker than the hair at the top.

"I can't do that anymore," he finally said.

"Do what?" I asked, unable to stop a small smile from creeping on my face.

"Become a rage-a-holic. I have to lose that," he said shaking his head. "The client's mom just gave me an earful. And she's right."

"What did she say?" I asked.

"She called me a potty mouth and told me I needed to pull it together. And I know she's right. I'm having a kid. My wife is pregnant. I don't want my daughter to see me like that."

"Well, you're having a boy," I said and laughed.

"What do you mean?" he said smiling weakly, almost as if he just became self-aware of his behavior on the street.

"Well, you have high testosterone. I think that means, boy. Or does it mean girl? I can't remember." I said looking upward trying to remember.

"You think I have high T?" he said quizzically.

"Well let's see: muscle bulk, check; receding hairline, check; hair trigger temper, check; and excess body hair," I say, pointing at his hair-covered meat hooks. "I bet we could bottle your blood and sell it to GNC."

He laughed hard as if the small joke disrupted his thoughts. It was hard to believe this was the same person who minutes ago wanted to impale a man with car parts. "You noticed I'm losing my hair, huh? You B****," he cursed at me. But not in the previously displayed anger, but with the playful weary acceptance that he would soon be bald.

"Listen, you'll be fine. No one is going to make fun of you man. No one wants to have their car mirror put in their butt," I laughed. He cast a truly terrifying figure when upset which I learned was instant and often.

"Hey, I'm getting better, man. No one called the cops. It was good day," he protested.

"Called the cops, does that happen?" I asked.

"It happened last week. It's a long story. I tried to pull a man out of his car through his window. The cops were called but I was not arrested. But today I didn't lay hands on him. I'm growing, man," he almost beamed, truly proud of himself.

Well, I guess measurement of growth depends on where you are starting the measurement. But if the bar is "Was I arrested?" well then, progress was made; because, well, he was not arrested.

Rob from Quebec, Canada is a very nice guy, unless you cross him by parking across the street from him and refusing to move when he asks you to.

I have heard that the key to happiness is setting achievable goals and then reaching them. Set your goals slightly higher than where you are currently. For some people that will be finishing your PhD, for another losing a little weight, going from 230 pounds to 210 pounds. For some people that will be no felony assault charges filed for the week.

Don't compare yourself to others, baby steps.

How was your day today? Did anyone call the cops on you? No? Sounds like a good day to Rob. He would be proud of you.

Let it Go

We are packing the client's dead plants. Well, that's not entirely right. They are not all dead, some are just dying. There are at least a dozen plants. One of them is already dead but he wants it packed, so we will. But he should really let it go. I have not packed too many men's plants. Plants are rare for men, more rare than mirrors. Last week we packed for two guys who were roommates in a 2000 square foot condo and there was not a mirror between them.

"No mirror to pack, right?" I ask, already knowing the answer.

"Why would we have one, bathrooms always have mirrors?"

Fair enough.

It's fine by me, plants and mirrors do not travel well. They are merely stacked at the back of the truck, roped in, and fingers crossed. What these two bachelors do have is a collection of swords, which is weird for a couple of reasons:

1. We do not live in medieval times.
2. It is not clear that these two have the upper body strength to wield these weapons.

Upon seeing the swords, Gav who is working with me today says, "I should get a sword." My opinion of him just drops dramatically.

"What would you do with it?" I ask in disbelief.

"I mean, I'd keep it on a shelf in my room."

Gav is a millennial. On the way to the job, I drive and he is 100% engrossed in his phone. He is from Vancouver. We get a lot of Canadian movers because we are paid off-the-books and he is not legally able to work in this country.

"I want to get done by 5:00 today. I want to go play basketball," he continues after enlightening me with his sword idea.

"Oh cool," I say, attempting small talk while sweating profusely. For whatever reason, I have started sweating immediately upon lifting the first bits of furniture. "Where are you playing?"

"Oh, a park," he says avoiding eye contact.

"Oh cool, with anyone I know?" I ask. I am not really interested, merely trying to fill the time with idle chatter.

"Uh, it's mostly younger guys," he pauses, "I guess you could come if you want?"

Ouch, that was one of the most begrudging invitations that I can ever recall getting. "It's ok," I say. He looks relieved but truly it's a win-win. I have seen him play basketball. It's a lot of slapping at the basketball while looking down and performing a disjointed lumbering move.

His lack of coordination is not something I celebrate, as sometimes it has caused me pain. On a past move, we parked a truck on a hill, a very steep hill. It was a struggle to push the dollies up the slope. A dolly got away from Gav and rolled down the hill hitting me squarely in the shins. An accident for sure, but a very frustrating accident that I would not like repeated. This loss of control is a metaphor for how he plays basketball, the dolly being the ball.

This client is moving out to the country. (I'm not sure if anyone told them there will be plenty of plants in the country. Most living freely without their little pot prisons.) They are moving to 7 Union Schoolhouse Rd, Mendham, NJ. It is about an hour and a half outside of Manhattan, west into New Jersey. The house they are moving to was built in 1809 and was previously a bank. A bank from 1809 sounds exciting. It's not. You might picture a saloon-like wooden structure with metal bars on the inside. It's not that. Instead, picture a two-level building on the side of a hill. In front of the house is a winding road and on the other side of the road, a stream.

This is truly a beautiful location in August. In February it is going to be cold and boring. This pandemic has caused people to move out of the city at almost any cost. Who can blame them?

My day started at 6 a.m. I made it to the truck rental place by 6:45. The company has reserved a truck for me, and I use the word company in the loosest way possible. If by company we can refer to an organization where no one knows anyone else's last name for tax reasons, then this is a barely functioning company. On this fine morning I give my driver's license to the attendant and he slips back into his little booth, the door closing behind him. After about 15 minutes he reemerges.

"The credit card on file has been turned down," he says, in a heavy accent. There are so many accents in NYC that not having an accent is really the accent.

This is the third time this month that the company's credit card has been turned down. It is frustrating to get up at 6 a.m. to get to work, stand in line at the truck rental place and then be told that the credit card on file isn't working. And there is always a reason. "I'm getting a new card today, as the last one got lost" or "It got demagnetized by my phone." At this point, the boss may as well say his dog ate it.

I am not going to put down my credit card for the rental. I am still owed by the company for the last rental. That's minus $300 for JJ's car.

I start making calls. First to the leader of this job to tell him what's happening. Then to the office. "Hey Kirk, just put down your card on the rentals again, we will reimburse you."

Ah, no, that is not something that interests me in the least, I don't want to, you lunatic, is what I'm thinking. But what I actually say is, "No, thank you."

There is a pause at the other end, then an argument pointing out the credit card points I would get if I use my card. As I mentioned I love frequent flyer miles, but I'm still owed from the last one and the thought of putting down a card on a 30-foot truck to be driven through the city making me 100% liable is holding less and less appeal. The offer of letting me charge the truck to my card is one that I am offered at least once a month, and only because their credit cards are constantly declined. If only there was a way to remedy the situation, by perhaps, I don't know, paying your bills on time?

When the call ends, the office is frustrated with me and I wonder if I am going to be fired, but I just play dumb. "No thank you, not interested." Playing dumb is one of my strongest moves, and given my face, it could almost be labeled typecasting. Just pay your bills every month so we don't have to play this charade.

I wait at the truck rental lot for over an hour. Eventually another credit card is called in by the office.

The last time that happened was on a move to Connecticut, and it also cost us an hour. We had been driving up to Bristol, Connecticut, the sports mecca--the home of ESPN. I was more than a little excited about it.

I remember watching ESPN in my late teens. I was in boarding school and there was a set up in Ecuador involving a satellite dish the size of a hotel room. Our dorm had five players of the varsity basketball team, and we watched Sports Center religiously. In the dorm we would vote every hour to see what channel we would watch, majority rule. At 8 p.m. every night, whoever was watching TV would get outvoted and we would see whatever incredible feat Bo Jackson or Michael Jordan had done that day.

The girls in the dorm dominated the TV all day on Saturday until 8 p.m., when we would descend like a band of baboons and vote to watch sports. There was only one TV in a dorm that housed 30 kids. Every hour, at the top of the hour, whoever was in the TV room voted on what to watch, you had to be present to vote. We always had the votes for that one 30-minute window. We had done some politicking and coerced Obie Manley, who only cared about Star Trek, to join us. We told him if he voted for sports, we would vote for Star Trek which started at 8:30 after Sports Center. After our show, we would stay and vote for Star Trek and then leave before the opening credits from Star Trek even started. The girls would get mad at us, but those were the rules. It was a crude, yet efficient voting bloc, not unlike the Eastern bloc ice skating judges or the more watched Eurovision Song Contest.

Well, that day on the way to the move, I would get to see the building where those highlights were edited, and where Chris Berman had for the first time yelled “Back-back-back-GONE” or “HE-COULD-GO-All-the-way!" in his staccato.

That Connecticut move required driving two moving trucks up to a warehouse where two pods had been stored, unloading those two pods into the two trucks, then driving them to Stamford, Connecticut. Pods are units, similar to truck containers that people use to move. The advantage is that the pods can be dropped off at people’s houses and loaded, then driven to the new location and unloaded. This client, for some reason, wanted us to unpack the pods, load them into two trucks and then drive to the new location. Maybe his money was burning a hole in his pocket, cause it was clearly wasteful, but that was not my concern. I am the help, seen but not heard. I would gladly oblige and help this fool and his money part.

We arrive up in Bristol around 11 a.m. Connecticut is a beautiful place to visit. I had lived there a few years in the early 2000s. The changing of the seasons from summer to winter involves that famous New England change in foliage. It brings out the leaf peepers who come to see the trees with their leaves painted bright reds and yellows. This beauty blinds people to the sub-zero temperatures that are just around the corner. Summer and fall are great. But winter is long.

We start to unload the pods that have been in storage for six months. There are many dubious items, including a couple of filthy rugs, several cheap plastic Christmas trees, and a bag of charcoal. Why someone would want to move charcoal, store it, and then move it again? I have no idea.

"I can't believe she said that to me," Andre, my unloading buddy, continues. He is detailing a story about his ex telling lies about him and trying to figure out why she would do that. Andre is in great shape. He was constantly at the gym pre-pandemic. Now that the gyms are closed, he is out in the street jumping rope and doing pull-ups off of scaffolding in the city like it's the most normal thing to do. Anything to continue to polish that exterior. I don't blame him; exterior is always easier to change than a tarnished interior.

As he describes the relationship, it occurs to me. This girl is not reacting to Andre, but like all of us, working through her own things.

It seems to me that people's insults are not always about us, but the result of processing things that have happened to them. Sometimes, these interactions are reflections of what they have experienced in their childhood. Those insults are not about you and you don't have to receive them. You can choose to just let them roll off you, "like water off a duck's back," my mom would say. You don't have to be insulted. Your words may have triggered something deep inside them, touching a wound that has not yet healed.

I should have said this to Andre, but I thought of it later. What I actually said was nothing. Instead, I continued to move tacky lawn furniture into the truck.

"And then she called me a narcissist and said I'm petty. She was the one who spent my money and then complained about ...," Andre's words cascaded out of his mouth. Based on his tone and how agitated he became, he really liked this girl. But it was not going to work. He had begged her to forgive him. She said no.

You are an extra in the play of their life. They are the protagonist and you will always be a supporting or periphery player. Their feelings will always be the backdrop to how they interpret life. Both the positive and the negative. The positive things they tell you are often a reflection of themselves as well. Something in them is triggered by something in you.

I should have said that to him. But instead I kept sorting through more crap in the pod. These items are not my items. Just like other people's personal baggage, I hold no responsibility for these things. These items were chosen by another. Each person individually makes their own choices and you are responsible for only your choices and mistakes. Your validation or worth does not depend on other people's opinions. You cannot control that. You control your own effort and attitude. That's it. Someone has to be the villain in their story and it is not going to be them. Never take credit or blame for the choices they make. Neither are yours to take.

But don't close your heart. You can love again. You can even say the words "I love you." You can ask for what you need. They can choose to give it to you or not. But you have to let some stuff go.

These are the things I should have said to Andre, but I didn't. Instead, I lifted things from one place to another, and from that place to another, finally to be taken to another place.

It costs us to hold on to grudges and hurts. Yet some still hold on to bitterness and pain like this client is holding on to this bag of charcoal.

"I'm going to do it," Gav's voice jolted me back to the present. "I'm getting a sword."

I nodded as I placed a box down on the edge of the truck. I wiped the sweat off my face with the sleeve of my shirt. Clouds were rolling in and it was humid.

There was so much I should have said to Andre about love and loss and trying to heal. But there's nothing I could say to Gav. You can't stop people from buying swords if they want to buy swords. They are going to buy swords.

Blue Gatorade

"Hey, we are going to pay you back for the truck rental today. Just take it out of the money the client gives you. Also, you're going to love this guy you're working with," Carlos is telling me on the phone.

I am the new guy so he doesn't have to sell me too hard, but he has been partnering me with a lot of bums this summer. He knows it and I know it.

"Hey man, I know I'm new but please just let me work with some of the good guys," I ask. There is a marked difference between the quality of the guys in the crew. Some move people's furniture carefully and others will show up high and try to pick fights with everyone.

"No man, I get it, you are going to love this guy, he's great. You're going to love him, his name is Rufat. He's new but he works so hard."

Carlos goes on and on about how hard Rufat is going to work and I agree, ok that's fine.

The next day, I am waiting in the truck at 7a.m. with Andy, when who should walk around the corner, but Big Sean— wearing shoes.

"Hey guys." he says. "Scoot over," he says to me.

"What? No man, we are waiting for Rufat," I smile, thankful that I am not working with Big Sean again.

"I am Rufat," Big Sean says. "That's my last name."

My face drops. Carlos has tricked me again; I fell for it. I scoot glumly over to the middle seat and just pray he keeps his shoes on for the day.

We load the truck and get on our way to the drop off.

"I'm just saying, you're wrong," Rufat says with the authority normally reserved for someone twice his age. Rufat, 27, was born in Baku and moved to NYC 15 years ago. Baku is on the Caspian Sea, and for some reason, I have wanted to go there for more than 20 years, but haven't made it yet.

Somehow, I got dragged into a discussion about religion 15 minutes into a four-hour drive. It is going to be a long ride in a tiny, tin truck cab. There is something refreshing and endearing when someone intelligent, whose life is going smoothly says, "it seems to me" or "in my experience." By the same token, there is something jarring about someone whose life is in chaos, yet, they not only have all the answers for themselves, but have the confidence and conviction to make sure you know, that they know, that you're wrong. And this conviction and attached dismissiveness does not lie exclusively with fervent followers of the major religions. An atheist can be just as evangelistic about their convictions as an evangelical.

The juxtaposition of the blatant disarray of how they live with the confidence with which they tell you how to live is grating. Or more simply, it is funny that they think they know everything when you can see that they don't. Case in point, I'm driving the truck, because you don't know how to drive.

It really is my fault. I know better than to have discussions about religion. I've never heard a discussion about religion end with one person going, "that's a great point, I had never thought of that". It's never been a fruitful exercise. Plus, there were clues that today's conversation might not be that enlightening while loading up the truck. During the load, I offered to get us drinks from the local bodega during a break.

"You want some water or Gatorade or something?" I ask.

"Yeah, Gatorade," the Caspian native replies.

"Cool, what flavor?"

"Ah, get me blue flavor and if they don't have that, white."

There are least five blue flavors. Can you taste color?

The drive during this spirited discussion about religion is in a fully loaded 30-foot truck--the contents of a household being moved to Southborough, Massachusetts from Brooklyn. It's a young couple with an infant baby making a big move from a three-floor walk-up in Park Slope to a boarding school called St. Marks. The school looks like a stand-in for a Harry Potter set. Complete with Tudor style buildings that include the bricks, exposed beams and even the odd tower. It is summer so the school is empty. The wind is blowing and there is an eerie silence. The campus is surrounded by forests and there is a desolate serenity to it. We back into a loading dock, all 30 feet of the truck making it down to the landing. It has been storming the last few days, but today is clear. The sky is open, and the wind is cutting through the trees, making the rustling sound city people don't recognize the first time they hear it. The trees are all you hear. There are no car horns, no guys yelling in the bodega.

The school was founded by Joseph Burnett who was born 200 years ago. Mr. Burnett made his fortune perfecting Burnett Vanilla Extract, the first or at least the finest vanilla the U.S. had to offer in the 1800s. He was an actual chemist and pharmacist who offered a product that would become world famous and build him a fortune. Burnett Vanilla Extract proved to be a much bigger success than his Burnett's cocaine product which promised to "stimulate healthy vigorous hair growth...and restore lost hair" but was in fact, mostly alcohol, coconut oil and cocaine. Restore hair? Probably not. Work for the famed expression, *hair of the dog*? Probably. In his free time when he wasn't running his cocaine business, Mr. Burnett founded an Episcopal church in Boston, and later, St. Marks. Somehow at the time, these two ventures did not contradict each other.

A caretaker eventually came to the loading dock to meet us. She was dressed as an actual schoolmarm, completing the outfit with a very time-appropriate face mask. What did she actually look like? I have no idea; I couldn't pick anyone out of a lineup these days as many faces are covered.

She greets us warmly and then guides us inside. We walk down the underground labyrinth of tunnels and doors 50 yards deep into the bowels of the building. We eventually reach a service elevator that was probably inaugurated during Woodrow Wilson's administration. It has two doors; both have to be closed manually. First, there is the completely exterior door that opens horizontally, with doors emerging from the top and from the bottom, coming together about waist high that have to be closed by pulling on a red rope. Then there is a second wooden gate that is lowered down from the ceiling. Only when both doors are closed will the buttons work. There are only two buttons, one going up and one coming down. There are no buttons to indicate what floor you are at, you stop based on your best guess. There is a window in the outside door that lets you see the passing floors, that is your only clue. A few times, I stopped too low to get the dollies off the elevator and had to close the gates and start over.

Blue Gatorade and I start to unload the truck. We take the furniture that needs to be assembled up first. That way Andy, who is the crew leader today, can stay in the apartment and begin to reassemble the furniture.

Among the client's belongings, there are two unusual chairs that I can't figure out if they are functional or just decorative. The bottom half is normal and looks like a standard IKEA kitchen chair. The top half of the back of the chair is three feet high. I am curious to see how it feels to sit in the chair.

"I wonder if these are for sitting on?" I ask Rufat as he hands them to me.

"Yeah, I'm sure they are. Try it. I think they make them for tall people."

"Are you sure?" I ask, uncertain.

"Yeah, yeah, I think I saw it online. Just sit on it, see how it feels." He sounds very confident.

I sit down as gingerly as my 210-pound frame can and lean back. I hear a creak. These are decorative chairs. I hop up and act as if I was not just sitting on a work of art.

"Huh, that's weird, maybe not," he offers. Maybe not indeed.

Rufat stacks the boxes from the truck onto dollies and I take them up the timeworn elevator to one of the spires of this off-brand castle. As I unload the boxes, I see Andy lying on the floor on his back, wrench in hand bolting the sectional couch back together.

Andy got engaged last week. It is his second or perhaps third time around the marriage block. He was married briefly three years ago to a fellow comic that I know. Then, in his words, both their careers and their drinking took off, and their marriage exploded. Since then, they have both gotten sober and turned their lives around.

"The key to a happy marriage is to cheat on your wife immediately. Then you never resent her," he tells me.

"What do you mean?" I ask, as this contradicts all the advice ever given to me.

"Well, if you cheat on her, then when she treats you badly, you don't resent her. You think 'yeah, she's being mean to me now, but I cheated on her, so it's really not that bad compared to what I did.'"

I smile and shake my head laughing. "So, to be clear, you don't resent her because you deserve it?" I ask, still confused.

"Yeah, kind of. I think you just are willing to put up with a lot more, if you know you already cheated on her."

With advice like this, I feel like I'm getting a small glimpse why this will be his third marriage before the age of 35. That advice is sure to unleash a personal hell for him when his new wife finds out.

Andy's marriages have been so quick that they remind me of the Nikah mut'ah or pleasure marriages that are practiced by the Shia Muslims in the Middle East. Originally, pleasure marriages were designed so a traveling merchant, who might spend months in a town, could marry a divorcee or widow for the length of his stay. Then when he departed, they could dissolve the marriage. It is now used by young people for long weekends, or in Andy's case, seven months, which was the length of the last one. Although as far as I can tell, the wedding was in Thousand Oaks, not Dubai.

I read once that over 70% of third marriages end in divorce, which if you're consistently cheating on your partner could explain that statistic.

We settle into the drive home. I'm driving, which leaves my companions with ample time and energy to spout off advice on a variety of subjects. Despite not having successful relationships, they are both experts. Being $40,000 in debt doesn't stop Andy from dispensing financial advice. His latest suggestion to me is to get rid of my car, which is paid for, and lease a new one. That advice would cost me several thousand dollars with very limited added benefits. But he is convinced this is a good financial move.

Rufat has very strong opinions on comedy despite never working at any of the comedy clubs in the city, or in any city to be frank. He also knows a lot about getting on TV, which he has also not yet done.

But the advice is not limited to these areas. Both Andy and Rufat wax elegantly on a variety of subjects that they have very limited knowledge of while I am their hostage driving them back to the city.

People just love to give unsolicited advice, regardless of their own personal lack of success. The more unqualified they are, the stronger the opinion they have.

I start to say something to rebut a particularly silly idea that one of them thinks about women. The idea would surely infuriate their girlfriends. As I do, I catch a glimpse of myself in the mirror and think, "I would really resent getting advice from someone like me," so I stop myself before giving them my little insight.

My dad always said, "Free advice is worth what you pay for it." I do know giving people unsolicited advice usually falls on deaf ears. They say people will only listen to your advice when they are ready to receive it.

They will figure it out, but I'll let them do it on their own time.

Good luck, boys. Hell hath no fury like a woman scorned.

Be Like Berlin

Today we are an hour late and it's pouring rain. The rain started late in the afternoon yesterday. The thunderstorms were beautiful to watch from indoors. Watching them from the outdoors in the pouring rain, not as much fun.

Today, I am part of a two man crew and we have three moves scheduled. The rain has made traffic a mess and the truck wouldn't even start for about 20 minutes. This truck is diesel and has a problem, the coil needs to heat up before it will turn over. Additionally, it has another problem which is, it's scrap and needs to be junked. The company trucks are driven by everyone and most of the crew drive them like they are stolen. It's almost as if they think they are in the video game GTA and the harder they drive them, the more points they get. Clip a mirror? 20 points. Back into a tree? 30 points. Leave the cab full of trash and smelling like a high school gym locker? No points; that's just par for the course. This is an International brand truck and is a dark green. This vehicle should have been discarded years ago but it has sentimental value to the owner, it's one of the first ones he bought.

Today, I am with Dwayne, an artist, who paints and sculpts. He is 5′10″ with very short hair. His medium frame hides his beer gut very well. He likes to, ironically, wear camouflage patterned jackets and pants, even though he is a pacifist.

"There is no better time to not be running a small business," he tells me and then continues. "I don't want the stress of running a business. Man, I'd rather just move heavy things. And get my money. Maybe it will get like Berlin. I remember when I was living in Berlin. Things were so cheap."

"Yeah, I remember they had apartments for 80k in the early 2000s," I say, remembering a trip I had taken to the fatherland. At that time, we were living in Sweden. When I tell people that, their question is always, "Where in Sweden?" When I answer "Edsbyn," they say, "Never heard of it."

Then I say, "What cities do you know in Sweden?"

Stockholm is always the answer. Well, my answer is not Stockholm. We were living about 4 hours north of there. The people from Stockholm would insult the people living up north by calling us pig farmers, which is an oddly specific insult that probably hits some people harder than others. Edsbyn was famous for winning the bandy championships for years (bandy is similar to hockey, but played with a ball, not a puck). It is also famous for having a giant red chair at the entrance of the town. In 2004, I was working out of the UK and would fly home to Sweden most weekends. My mother-in-law had cancer and had gone home to Sweden for care. I transferred to the London office commuting from Edsbyn. My job was to manage a network of vendors in Europe, and one of the trips was to Berlin. At the time, Berlin was an artist's paradise. Back then, the city was dominated by the grey concrete block style housing that permeated all of eastern Europe. The architecture served as evidence of their not so distant shared history with the USSR. The buildings may have been grim, but the arts were experiencing a renaissance, of which Dwayne had been part of.

"There was this one scene, man, just on the east side. I had some great times there, man." Dwayne reminisced. His eyes stared out the windshield to the rain pelting our beat-up truck. We had arrived in the lower east side of Manhattan, Alphabet City, and it was time to get out of the truck and start the first of three moves for the day.

"I'll go check in with the client. See if you can find a parking spot." And with that, he was off, jogged back to reality by the prospect of manual labor. I was now assigned the task of trying to parallel park a giant truck in Manhattan in a monsoon. There were no spots, so I parked around the corner next to a fire hydrant and then walked to the back of the truck.

Dwayne came back with the scoop. This lady has most of her belongings in plastic bags. The company has a policy of only allowing boxes, not bags. However, Dwayne is in charge today and he is a soft touch and isn't comfortable pushing back given that we are an hour late to start the job.

"Man, if we had been on time, I would have crushed this lady, but we are an hour late. That's not good customer service."

I nod. What do I know, man, I'm just driving the truck. All I know is that boxes can be stacked on a dolly. You can stack 6 boxes on each dolly and one person can push two dollies at a time down the street. The plastic bags cannot be stacked. They cannot go on dollies. They can easily rip and stuff can fall out, in the rain. If you get one thing from this book, it's be kind; ok, two things. The second thing is don't move your belongings in garbage bags. This move is on 165 Attorney Street, a very narrow street. Parking the truck around the corner means that the move was down three flights of stairs and then another 200 feet down the street and then around the corner, in a torrent. After loading the truck, driving it about a mile and carrying the things up to a much nicer place, we move on to the second job.

The second move is for a couple on 105 W 29th. They have absolutely everything boxed up. There is a service elevator and no steps, but more importantly, no bags. It's all in boxes. They must have read the last paragraph.

"See, these people have their s*** together. These people are Type A, man. The first lady is probably a boss, she thinks she's Type A. She's moving to Gramercy Park; she has money, but she's dumb. She's probably screwing up at the job. We sent out so many emails and she ignored them. The boxes she did have were overpacked. It says right in the email. 'If you can't lift it, we shouldn't have to lift it.' You think she could carry those boxes down?" Dwayne says all this to me.

But does he say it to the client? The lady who packed the boxes? Nah. The boxes were well over 60 pounds each, half of this lady's body weight. She was not going to be lifting them. I assume he is being rhetorical, because he continues, "Nah, man, no way she can."
He's not wrong, she could not have carried one of the boxes down the stairs. But it is odd to hear an artist so enamored with Type A people.

The second move went smoothly. The couple was from Minnesota and they are just happy to be alive. They have that contagious energy and, what's that called? Oh yeah, joy, and joy is infectious. I even hear an "Oh yeah, you betcha" thrown in by the client when we ask if they are excited to be moving. They are moving to a beautiful place in Dumbo right on the water, which is going to be an adjustment after living in Chelsea.

The third move is a doctor. I know he is a doctor cause he told me about it five minutes into meeting him. "I'm a doctor, I ran the Javits Center. I was working with two and three-star generals." I nod as I lift a couch on to the truck. I don't know if that is true, but I do know that everything he owns is covered in cat hair. People love their cats and cats love to shed hair. I knew there was a cat when I saw the cat tree and cat condo on the packing list. I saw it soon enough to take my nasal steroids and eye steroids. I know some of you are probably struggling to contain your excitement with me talking about a subject as sexy as allergies. What can I say? I'm a provocateur.

The doctor was maybe 32 years old and could stand to lose a few pounds. He had a well -trimmed beard and gave a long, unrequested explanation of how important his job was. I don't know. I believe him. I mean, he's a doctor, and he said it's important, so there is that. He was a nice guy and seemed to really love his wife and more importantly his cats. Really, the more he talked, the less I felt like I knew him. He was moving within Morning Side, that tippity top part of Manhattan on the west side of the island. Technically, the northern part of the Bronx, but separated by a river, so still Manhattan. The building he was moving to was on Riverside Drive, a busy four-lane road where there is no parking. Also, it's on a hill. We double parked; I put my hazards on, pulled the mirrors in and started unloading cat furniture. There was the cat condo and two cages. I know grown men with less furniture than this cat, shoot I have less furniture than this cat. And a rug that was clearly their territory as it was covered in cat hair as well as several other items that smelled like the kitties had marked their territory.

The doctor continued his soliloquy. "Yeah, after residency, I just couldn't find a job that I liked. I mean, residency was hard and then there was just nothing that moved me. I just kept plugging away, plugging away and eventually I got something. It will happen for you too, man. Someday, maybe you'll own your own moving company!" I appreciate the encouragement; but bite your tongue good doctor. I have no interest in having my own business of moving people's garbage.

But, he's not wrong. If you got laid off with the economy taking a hit, you have to remember, things will not always be this down. The tide goes out and comes in. When the tide is out, it is sometimes hard to visualize the water ever coming back, but it does. It always does. During the earthquakes with their accompanying tsunamis, all the water is pulled into the sea and the bottoms of the ocean are laid bare. All its depths and secrets are exposed to the world. But, the water does return and your blessings can come roaring back as well.

That the water could be pulled out (like most tragedies) isn't even considered until it happens. Then with hindsight, it seems inevitable, but the water will be back. As unlikely as it seems, the water will return. The tide will come back in and bring with it the life that it took from you. It will be back; you will be back. Prepare for it or don't. It will pour back in; you don't have to want it to come back. You don't have to will it. You don't have to push or wish for it. It will return. Will you be ready for it? Will you welcome back the rush of life?

Take this time to line up your dominos, there are things you can do when you have this kind of down time to build. Build your career, your life, your relationships.

Don't allow the rising tsunami of blessings to overwhelm you. It is coming. The life and energy that was taken from you will return. Just as things were taken from you unfairly, undeservedly, things will be given to you undeservedly. You will be blessed, unfairly. You will someday receive. Prepare, don't wallow in your despair.

Berlin was down. It endured decades of neglect and decay. After being a gem of Europe, it was disowned and abandoned for a time. But it came roaring back, all the way back and some. Take this time to invest in yourself while you, like Berlin, are down.

Someday there will be parking, and not on hills and maybe even cold drinks after the job.

"To every man there comes in his lifetime that special moment when he is figuratively tapped on the shoulder and offered a chance to do a very special thing, unique to him and fitted to his talents. What a tragedy if that moment finds him unprepared or unqualified for that which would be his finest hour."

Winston Churchill

Dazed and Confused

Lee is point today. Point is just a fancy way to say "the boss."

Who is Lee? He is a dead ringer for a disheveled looking Dax Shepard, the actor. He is from Colorado and looks the part of a drugged-out stoner. He is tallish and can definitely cross that six-foot tall threshold that so many lie about. Why tell someone you are six feet tall when you will eventually meet them in person? Once you are face to face, your physical stature will be obvious because, well, you are there physically. But Lee doesn't have that problem.

I arrive at 6:45 a.m. and I see Lee hanging out at the back of the truck eating a deli bagel sandwich. The truck has a softball size hole in the rear of the box where someone obviously didn't see an electric pole and the telephone equipment hanging from it.

"Hey, nice to meet you, I'm Kirk," I offer.

"Lee," he says with a big smile and takes a big bite of his sandwich slathered in mayo. "We are waiting for Jared," he tells me with a mouth full of mayo sandwich.

Eventually, Jared saunters up. He is literally strolling up like he is not 15 minutes late. He is wearing all black including leggings, iced coffee and donut in hand.

Lee has finished his sandwich by now and is drinking a brown beverage that he has mixed out of a powder. "Jared?" Lee offers.

Jared takes out his AirPods, like we just interrupted his early a.m. stroll through this bad part of Brooklyn.

"Sorry, are you Jared?" Lee asks apologetically.

"Oh, yeah," Jared confirms as if somehow surprised by the question.

"Great, let's roll, I'll drive," Lee replies.

"I thought I was supposed to drive?" I ask, as I have always driven with this company.

"Not today; it's your lucky day," he replies.

We climb in the truck and I quickly realize why Lee wants to drive. The driver seat is separated from the other seat by the gear shift and an empty space of about six inches. The other two riders must share a bench seat, and there is not a divider between them. Jared is a wide man, maybe six feet tall but easily 280 pounds and not going to easily fit on the bench with another person.

"Hey, you mind if I get the window?" Jared asks.

Of course I mind. I'm the tallest man here, with the longest legs, and I was here before him. That's what I think, but what I say is, "Ok, I guess. We can switch off." I squish into the middle seat and immediately regret it. Jared is spilling over on to me with his legs manspread wide open; I feel like I am being violated.

"Buddy, you have to close your legs a little," I tell him.

"Oh, right, sorry," he offers and closes his legs an inch. One inch. Our legs are still touching from the hip to the calf. The way he's spreading out his legs, you would think he has elephant gonads. I'm already tired of this drive and Lee hasn't even started the truck yet. This is going to be a long day.

I sit, pinched between two strangers, knowing it can't get any worse, when it does. Lee pulls out his rolling papers and tobacco and a little something extra. He rolls it and then without asking if we mind, he lights it, takes a long drag and then starts the truck. I give him a look of disbelief. It's just after 7 a.m. and I am not eloquent, but my look says, "You have to be joking."

He interprets my "you have to be joking" look, as a look of craving and holds his little cigarette out to me, while holding his breath and raising his eyebrows. I shake my head no. Before I can articulate the word no, Jared reaches over me, brushing up against my arm and chest and grabs it.

"Yeah, man, let's do it," says Jared who has now found his voice. It's a miracle. All he needs to speak is a quick hit from a stranger while still in a parked truck in Brooklyn.

"Come on, man," I say. "At least let's drive to get some air circulating in here. I'm allergic to the smoke."

"Oh yeah, let's do it," Lee replies as if without my prompt, we might have stayed there for hours. We start down the street with me, the guy who looks like a Mormon missionary, riding between these two Cheech and Chong stoner characters. The truck bounces along with us three like little popcorn kernels, every odd bounce landing Jared's unwelcome leg on me. I can feel my asthma start to kick in and hope I don't die. I left my inhaler at home along with my self respect.

We finally arrive at the first load site for the day. It's at 1571 Lexington Ave on the upper east side. It is the much dreaded and feared 5th floor walk-up. These buildings without elevators are a testament to the age of the city and to people's willingness to overlook the 100 feet vertical climb just to get to their apartment.

This apartment has two roommates who both booked movers the same day, the last day of their lease. In a strange twist, both roommates have hired movers from the same company. As a result, I know the other crew.

When we pull up to the building, I can see that the other crew is already there and loading the truck. One of the other crew members is Andre. He's bald, absolutely ripped, just turned 40 and is a known ladies' man. He works as a mover and then in his free time does additional exercise; he is one of the zero-percent-body-fat-people.

He was a fashion photographer for over 10 years and then gave it up (his words), which is code for he stopped getting work. Who knows? What I do know is that he has been talking passionately to a member of some sort of law enforcement.

"That's absolute crap," I can hear him yell at the officer who is getting back into a Chevy Impala.

"Buddy, that's the law, man."

"What happened?" I ask.

"I just got a ticket for putting some tape in the trash can!" he says, gesticulating wildly towards the public trash can.

"What do you mean?" I say, hoping for clarification.

"I guess, no business trash in public garbage cans. I'm going to fight it, man," Rob is waving his ticket while walking to his car. At this point, the officer has driven off and Lee has double parked our truck 100 feet up from the entrance in the only spot open. He is walking up to us slowly.

"They gave the super one too. Watch your truck, they tried to give me one for being double parked too," Rob says to Lee.

"I can sit in the truck," Jared volunteers, suddenly interested in the conversation.

"You couldn't move the truck. You don't even have a license. What could you do?" Lee replies in a moment of clarity.

"True, true," Jared disappointedly concedes and his hopes of sitting in the truck while we climb and descend five flights of stairs are dashed forever.

We ascend and descend the stairs, again and again, taking down things that would have ridden perfectly content in an elevator, if one was available.

The truck is loaded without a ticket, which is a win today. We walk back to the cab and as I start to get in, Lee gets his tobacco out and starts to roll again.

"I can drive too, if you want me to," I offer again for the third time today. Lee is the point, in charge of this move, so it's his call.

"Nah, I got it. I've had a month off, I'm ready to get back in the groove," he tells me. I don't know if this is the best way to prepare to drive trucks through Manhattan, with a performance inhibitor.

"Ok, if you're both going to smoke, I'm taking the window. I'm allergic to the smoke," I announce, expecting an argument from Jared.

"Ok, cool," Jared surprisingly agrees, perhaps realizing he's that much closer to the product. They smoke, I stick my head out the window to try to get as much clean air as possible. I'm winded from the steps and with my head out the window, I look like a Labrador covered in sweat and dust. They are both very excited about the cigarettes, and I try to start a conversation with Jared and see if he will use a full sentence.

"You working tomorrow?" I ask trying to fill the time.

"Nah, man. Not Saturdays. I take that day off," he says and then gets very serious and leans forward like he is telling me a secret. "Here is the thing man. I like to meet women and hang out. I do that on Saturday," he tells me.

That was the big secret. Yes Einstein, all single, heterosexual men like to hang out with women. Do you think Einstein had a brother who was not as a smart and his friends tried to burn him with, "You're no Albert," instead of, "You're no Einstein?"

The company has all the jobs on a shared Google Doc. The address on the app for the destination of this move is 329 E 87th. However, there is no 329 E 87th. Lee calls the client. He talks to her as we patiently await what comes next. He finishes the call and fills me in.

"Turns out it's 529 E 87th. And I think she told me that before, based on that call."

"What do you mean?" I ask.

"Well, I think I said, '329' E 87th, right?" and then she said, "529 E 87th," and then I said, "Right, 329 E 87th." With that he makes a pained wincing expression knowing he was in the wrong. I may have looked like a Labrador hanging out of the window, but this guy might be as smart as a bag of dog food.

"Hey, Kirk why you breathing so hard?" Jared asks me.

"I told you man. Asthma. Triggered by the smoke," I say, trying to be cool and hide my frustration.

We circle back again and find another parking spot. After our little mishap, the unload goes relatively smoothly. Jared, halfway through, tells us he's tired and takes a break to watch stories on Snapchat.

"Yo, she's mad fine," he comments, as I walk by him carrying plastic bins.

"Uh huh," I try to confirm, although I can't even see his screen with these bins towering over my head. I keep walking, as these bins are not going to walk themselves up the four flights.

We get back to the truck and you guessed it. Lee's back to rolling and I'm back to asking if I can please drive. No dice to the driving, but yes to the rolling, and yes to me getting the window.

The second job goes smoothly and we stop at Taco Bell before proceeding to the third job. Why Taco Bell? Cause we all have bad taste and no regard for our intestines.

We arrive at the third job a little after 6 p.m. and Lee goes back into his bag and starts looking for something. He finds his brown concoction in a plastic bag and starts to mix it with water.
"What is that?" I inquire.

"It's Kratom," he says like everyone has heard of that.

"What's that?" I ask honestly, having never heard of it.

"They use it in Indonesia. The workers do; I heard they use it in Egypt too. You can work for hours, man. It makes you strong."

"Is it bad for you?" I ask.

"No man, it's natural. It's made from a tree," he says that like it answers my question. Buddy, poison ivy is natural, and so is arsenic, but I will have neither, please and thank you.

"What's it taste like?" I ask.

"Oh man, it's terrible. It tastes like butt." As if we all know what butt tastes like.

Well, there you have it. A tree that tastes like a bottom, but makes you strong like a bull.
He continues to mix and drink. He makes a pained expression, as he downs it. It looks agonizing.

After his self-torture, we continue with the next couple. They are escaping Bushwick and heading to Greenpoint. The street in front of their house is covered with dog poo. People in the city love their dogs. But some people don't like picking up their dog's poo. The price is some neighborhoods look like a poo poo platter. I take a stray piece of cardboard and push the offending feces into dying grass surrounding a small tree. There you go little tree, all the fertilizer you can eat. All I need is to step in that, while carrying a 300 pound couch and fall into another pile, made by someone's "precious baby."

I heard once that in 1880, there were 150,000 horses drawing horse carts around this city, one of the early versions of public transportation. Each horse produced 22 pounds of manure a day, leading to millions of pounds of manure each day. There was so much manure, that it was a public nuisance and people could slip and fall in it. There was an entire department of sanitation dedicated to it in NYC. I heard, perhaps an apocryphal tale, that when cartoons were referencing the manure, they would insert banana peels into the show as the manure was thought too crass for children to see. Well, this street is a throwback to that earlier time and if it were a cartoon, this street would be covered in banana peels.

We load this nice couple's things and move them to Greenpoint, a quiet, Polish neighborhood that has become quite popular. We start unloading their things after 9 p.m. and it is already dark. At one point, Jared disappears. I wondered if he had gone home, but he wanders back with a candy bar and soda.

While Jared disappeared, Lee and I continue to unload the truck. I don't know if the Kratom was psychosomatic, but Lee is almost running back and forth from the truck to the apartment. We are now 14 hours in, and this maniac is almost sprinting. I wonder if in his mind, he is transferred to the jungles of Borneo with his bow and arrow and is hunting deer.

Jared eventually joins the group again and we finish unloading their things —it's around 10 p.m. I go to the back of the empty truck to remove the tape and fold the moving blankets that we have used. Lee jets back to the house. He eventually returns after we have finished folding everything.

We climb back into the truck and I await the smoke that has punctuated each of the other drives.
"You don't have no more cigarettes?" Jared asks sadly.

"No, sorry I'm out. But I can get you a beer. The client gave us a six pack. I already slammed one while you were closing the gate." Lee gives a sly smile, starting the truck.

Jared perks up after his initial disappointment.

I would roll my eyes, if I had the energy, as our Kratom/beer fueled driver speeds us off into the night.

I Got you Son

"Ahh crap," he yells out, although he doesn't say crap. This motley crew I am working with today is old school Brooklyn. These days, Brooklyn is cool and hipster friendly. But I and the other two guys on this job are old enough to remember when Brooklyn wasn't just hard. It was legitimately dangerous. Shoot, Sudanese warlords would have seen Brooklyn and admired the tenacity and violence right in the heart of one of the world's capitals.

I'm working hard on my patience. I have never been a patient person, but Rome wasn't built in a day and I'm working on it.

It's a moving day again, and I am standing at the back of the truck about to place my end of a couch on the truck bed. Tremain is standing on the back of the truck rearranging something to make room for this final piece of furniture, this couch. It has already been a long morning. We are moving a very well-matched couple out of the city from 535 W. 23rd right in the heart of Chelsea, just a few blocks from Madison Square Garden, home of the perennially terrible NY Knicks, to the country. The couple is dressed like they are modeling active wear from a fancy J. Crew catalog, with perfectly coiffed hair and matching tan colored outfits.

Tremain's profanity catches my attention and I look up to see something falling off the back of the truck and heading down towards me. I tried to move but am pretty much locked in place by this couch and only manage to move one of my legs out of the way. I am pinned in, specifically, I am holding the north end of an eight foot long sofa bed. It is pushing 400 pounds and we had just walked it down a very tight stairwell in a third floor walk-up. I was spent.

Today I am working again with Tremain. He has been working for this company for way too long. He hates this job but would never quit. He will work here until the bitter end. They will take him off this job in a body bag. There are few jobs in NYC that will pay hundreds of dollars a day, require zero education and allow you to get paid in cash at the end of the day. As long as this job meets these requirements, he's going nowhere. He is wearing the working man's version of golden handcuffs. He is over this job, but he will stay, resent it, complain about it, accidently drop things on me, but never leave.

I see the coffee table travel in slow motion off the truck, hit my leg just below the knee at an angle and scrape the skin off all the way down my shin, and then land on my foot.

"Ooooow," is what I yelled out, very loudly. It is not profound, but it is honest. "I'm putting this down," I announce to Dwayne who is carrying the south end of this beautiful, white couch that costs as much as a top end jet-ski.

I put the couch down quickly. A little too quickly. The coffee table that had fallen is still on my foot. In the process of lowering the couch I inadvertently placed it on the table, pinching my fingers. Specifically, the tip of my left middle finger. "I'm going to lose that nail," I yell out and quickly lift the couch back off of the table which is still resting on my foot.

"Tremain. Get. This. Table. Off. My. Foot." Apparently, when I am in pain, I over enunciate everything making myself sound like an English teacher who is being tortured. If I had been placed on the rack in the Middle Ages, I might as well have yelled, "Red leather, yellow leather," that ancient tongue-twisting exercise, delighting my college theater professor, Bob Abplanalp.

Tremain has a reputation for being slow, but when he wants to move, he moves. He was already off the truck and lifting the table off my leg. "I got you. I got you. I got you, son," he kept repeating. I hate it when people tell me they got me. The only thing I dislike more is when they tell me they "got you, son." Son? I'm old enough to be a very, very young grandfather. I'm older than you. If anything, I'm the dad here and you're the son. And like a dad, I am the one who is disappointed and angrily seething quietly.

Actually, the only thing that I dislike more than, "I got you, son" is when someone says it after dropping something heavy on me. Like a table. I'm not your son and you don't need to get me. But I do need you to stop dropping things on me and making me bleed. Do that and we are good.

I hop around for a few more seconds on my good, non-bleeding leg and close my eyes to try to control my emotions. Serenity now. Serenity now. You are not going to lose your temper, Smith, hold it together. I force a fake smile that involves scrunching my eyes together and lifting the corners of my mouth without showing any teeth. If I show my teeth it will look fake, but right now, it's hard to tell as most all of us, I have a mask on which I can hide behind when I am truly in physical or emotional pain.

I mentioned we are in Chelsea in Manhattan, on 24th Street between 10th and 11th Ave. Right in the heart of the city. As my leg throbs, I look up and can see part of The High Line. The High Line is a mile and a half elevated, linear park. It runs on the former New York Central train line on the West Side of NYC. An elevated oasis in this now concrete jungle. It starts in the Meatpacking District and terminates near the Javits Center. Roughly modeled on the French Coulée Verte René-Dumont or Promenade Plantée, The High Line is distinct in that it was built on top of an existing edifice. Specifically, it was built on top of an abandoned, above-ground rail line. It's a unique feature in an American city and probably owes some of the reason for its creation to the fact that it was cheaper to build a park on top of it than to demolish it.

I look down at my leg and can see the blood trickling down the shin. Starting at the knee, my blood is gathering steam by joining the sweat, and running down past the newly swollen flesh that is already starting to bruise. Hair, pulled out by the roots, has clumped together with the freshly detached skin. At the top of the foot where the leg meets the ankle, a chunk is missing. This is where the table rested, creating that quarter size hole in the skin where my leg meets my foot. Not a deep hole mind you, but a hole nonetheless.

I have always liked white shoes, but they prove to be a mistake with this job. The top of my white shoe and only slightly visible sock beneath, are now soaked with blood. The tongue of the shoe was bright red, but then diluted by sweat has become a harmless pink. I look up and see that in the interim my coworkers have gotten the couch on the truck while I was hopping around. Well, that's good at least.

"You ok? You ready to go?" Dwayne asks. Sympathy is not something this job has in abundance. I slowly nod. This was the last item and standing around is not going to help.

"Want me to get a Band-aid or something?" Tremain offers.

"For which part?" I ask looking down at the leg. My leg is scraped a good 12 inches, from below my knee to my ankle with several lacerations.

"Good point," he replies.

"I have hand sanitizer in my backpack," I say.

"Oh, cool," and with that he dismisses himself and heads to the front of the truck. Dwayne climbs up on the bed of the truck and pulls down the gate with the strap. I head around the truck to the driver's side. Today again, I am driving. The seats of this truck were wet this morning which is disgusting, what was the offending liquid? Your guess is as good as mine. To make yourself feel better just tell yourself it is rain, although it has not rained in a few days. I did however grab a moving blanket, the cleanest one I could find, and laid it down on the seat to soak up some of the filth before placing my hiney on it.

We are headed up to Mount Kisco today. Our exact destination is 115 Tripp Street, a beautiful house that has been updated. We start by taking a left on to 10th Ave. from 24th St. We head north on 10th Ave., cutting across one block east on 26th St., then left again headed north on 8th Ave. We stop at the Dollar Pizza place on 25th St. The swanky, new pizza spot on 8th and 29th St. that opened right before the pandemic, has already gone out of business. But this is NYC and a new pizza shop seems to open as another closes, the circle of life indeed. I get two cheese slices and a can of root beer for three dollars. Growing up in a religious teetotaler family where alcohol was strictly verboten, I remember ordering root beer with a special panache. Just saying the word beer in the context of a soda pop made me feel like a wild man. "One root beer, please. Hold the ice."

We eventually make it over to the East Side of town, up 1st Ave and over the Willis Bridge, that little forgotten stepchild of a bridge that you would completely forget about if it was not on your direct route. We make it to Expressway 87 and then to 95 continuing to venture north. As you may recall, commercial traffic is banned on the parkways in New York. I wish Google maps had a "exclude parkways" button however it does not. Additionally, commercial vehicles are not merely excluded from legally riding on parkways; they are also physically unable to. The trucks will literally not fit under many of these old stone bridges that were created for a different time, designed for horse drawn carriages, not for 30-foot Hino box trucks complete with a bleeding driver who might need a skin graft.

As always, 15 miles from the city, the panorama changes drastically. Stone edifices give way to greens and browns. The trees roll by beside us, taking up more and more of the view and filling my mind with thoughts of chucking it all in and moving to a cabin. But then what? Do I get WiFi at this cabin? Is there electricity? How about hot water? I'm weird about smells and could not live the rest of my life smelling like onions and potatoes. Do I live alone in the woods? Or is it nice enough to be able to convince a woman to come with me to live in stinky squalor.

Off the freeway, the road winds this way and that. Around bends, climbing and dropping until eventually we are at a beautiful house with a long gravel driveway. I turn the truck in, backend first, and small stones are kicked up by the tires as we curve around the house, in a slow loop.

I get out of the truck slowly, winching like a man twice my age. The hand sanitizer, dried blood, pulled out hair, and dead skin have dried in a messy paste. The still intact hair on my legs is abundant, very ape like, and has joined the matted mess. Now, my movements are breaking apart this disgusting cornucopia. Each step I take breaks up the new scab and starts the coagulation process all over. We start to unload the truck and I forget about my leg.

It is a beautiful day. The weather is perfect: mid 70s, low humidity. But it is a trap. As all true New Yorkers know, it's the kind of day New York lays out for you right before winter to trick you into forgetting that in a few months you will be miserable in its below freezing temperatures.

The client's house is a 4-bedroom, 5-bathroom former farmhouse built in 1880. It is updated but the contractor kept some of the original items, like the lights that jut out of the walls on the staircase in the house just below eye level. They are made to look like old gas lights including a bright red knob to control the gas, despite the fact the lights are all electric bulbs. A superfluous, but beautiful design touch perhaps being the very definition of art. Gratuitous and at the same time elegant and exquisite.

We begin unloading with the last things loaded onto the truck. Last in, first out, the couch.

"You want to do this couch?" I ask Tremain, secretly hoping he will say no.

"Yeah," Tremain says. He often says this, but he says it in a fake deep voice, the opposite of a falsetto. He is imitating the word and tone to a specific rap lyric, and it was enjoyable the first time I heard it. This is the 15th time he has said it to me today. It's definitely less fun than the first time I heard it, and it is now something I wish he would stop saying.

The couch is wrapped in blankets and then plastic wrap. I take the first end of the couch off of the truck, which means I will be backing up several flights of stairs. I would prefer to take the bottom position. The bottom position means you will shoulder more of the weight, but you can place it on your shoulder and just lift it. Just push, instead of pull. Backing up the stairs is hard for taller people because you end up leaning over the item and when it's covered in plastic and a little wet from sweat, it gets slick. It is a recipe for disaster.

We ascend the first flight of stairs uneventfully. Slowly, but steadily. We navigate the brutal tight corners and finally begin to climb the second set of stairs. Halfway up the stairs Tremain trips and starts to fall, pushing the couch up at me. I fall back still holding the couch wrapped in plastic which is now wet from sweat. As I start to fall, my neck and shoulder area catch a red nob from the light fixture.

"Ooow," I yell out, as I'm pinched between the wall, the fixture, and the couch. Additionally, I flinch when I hit the light bulb, searing a small but permanent burn on my neck. I have now been branded. The couch falls, sliding down my same tormented leg. Fresh blood now running down my leg, streaming into my already bloody sock and shoe, changing the color from the crimson and pink back to a bright red. The white couch is thankfully fully wrapped in plastic, protecting it from the gore.

"I got you, son. I got you," Tremain helpfully proclaims.

"Don't get me, get this couch off me," I couldn't help but say, in a tone less cool than I was trying to be. It sounds like I am in pain, which is the opposite of how I want to sound, cool and impervious to harm. I push the couch off of my leg and back in Tremain's direction and to his credit, he takes it, Termain is deceptively strong. I straighten back up, still holding the couch and we slowly begin to ascend this piece to its new home.

The rest of the unload goes smoothly. Nothing else is dropped on anyone and we methodically go through the truck, taking each item to its new spot.

In the end, the truck is emptied and furniture unwrapped. We get paid and get back on the road.

We take a slightly different route back to the city. On expressway 95, I am following a work van very closely. It is 6 p.m. and the highway is full. It is still light outside but the day is beginning to betray its plans to soon plunge us into darkness. As we barrel down the road our truck was perhaps 20 feet from the van in front of us. I was zoned out going through the motions, after a long grueling day, when I am snapped to life. There on the road, in the middle of my lane, is a squirrel. Still alive but it looked like it had been hit in its left front leg and shoulder. The image is burned into my mind.

I see it pinned to the road, right in the middle of the expressway. The van in front of me clears it without hitting it again and I clear it too, with the small animal's body lying on the road as the undercarriage of my truck passes over it harmlessly. But there it is in the road, with nothing to be done. There are cars all around me and traffic is heavy. Even if I could get over several lanes and pull off to the side and stop 300 feet down the road, I couldn't cross several lanes of very heavy traffic to remove the squirrel. All this is going through my mind when I see car behind me hit it cleanly, gruesomely putting it out of its misery.

It makes me think. Initially someone had hit the squirrel, accidentally. Without malice someone had injured it, damaged it; the squirrel's demise was in a manner similar to what happened to my leg, but much more severely. All the same, pain had been caused.

As I sit next to Tremain after our day of hijinks and pain, I realize sometimes we do things that hurt people. And we are sorry. And we say we are sorry, but that doesn't make the pain that they feel any less real. They are going to be in pain and suffer, because of a mistake we made. Sometimes we run into the danger and share in the blame, and in the process are run over by life.

But sometimes you will suffer and experience pain for the mistakes other people make, through no fault of your own. It's the savage human experience. Whether you are at fault or not, pain can be inflicted accidentally from one person to the next. Pain inflicted accidentally and unintentionally can still pack all the same ferocity as pain inflicted with malicious intent.

In the end we need to forgive those who inflict pain on us, particularly those who do so unintentionally. I say this to myself as much as to anyone else. It is not easy, but there is no other way. The squirrel can be angry at the car all it wants, but that will not help save its life or lost limbs. I can be upset with Tremain all I want, but it will not remedy my lacerated leg and ankle. The damage has already been done.

I should just forgive Tremain. I haven't, but I should, I have to, eventually.

I will, just not yet, just relax, I got you Son.

I'm in an Uber

I wake up to a woman crying and yelling. For a minute, I think I'm in trouble and then remember I can't be. I live alone. No wife, no girlfriend. I hate making a woman cry, especially when I'm not sure why it is happening. Ever make a woman cry? You feel terrible and you want them to know you feel terrible, but shoot, it's hard to sympathy cry. Sometimes I have to sit on one of my own balls just to shed a little tear.

I have been sleeping with my windows open. This week the temperature in New York City has significantly come down, a crisp 59 degrees tonight brings with it a welcome respite from the heat. Normally the open window ushers in a cool nightly breeze, but tonight it also ushers in shouting.

I check the time on my phone and it's 5:30 a.m. I don't have to wake up for another two hours. I look out of my first-floor apartment window to the street. I see on the sidewalk a woman wearing sweatpants and an oversized sweatshirt, yelling into her phone.

"Baby, no wait. I'm on my way," she yells into her cellphone. She is talking very loudly and I see a light go on across the street in the apartment directly opposite mine. I see the silhouette of another person in the window peering down at the action. I keep my light off in the hopes that I can soon go back to sleep.

There is a pause as the person in the street listens to the receiver. Then she continues.
"No, I'm already in the Uber, I'm a few blocks away." She was not in the Uber. She was right in front of me. Both nosy neighbor and nosy me can clearly see her.

"Go faster, I need to get there," she says, pretending to tell the imaginary driver. She is wearing a mask so I can't see what she looks like, but based on her clothes, I would guess late 20s or early 30s, but it's so hard to tell these days.

I close my window and lie back down. I try to relax but I can hear the muffled voice distinctly through the silence of the night. I stay as still as I can. I'm eavesdropping on a one-sided conversation. There is pleading and crying. After a few minutes, I head back to the window and watch. Guiltily. I know I shouldn't be listening, but I just can't stop myself.

A few minutes later a cab rolls up our street. She waves it down and gets in.

"Seventy and Second please," I think I hear her say.

She's going to the upper Eastside. As the vehicle drives away, I can still hear her yelling through the open windows of the car. And just like that, she's gone. I lie back down and drift off to sleep for several hours before heading off to pick up the moving truck.

The alarm on my phone jolts me awake and I sit straight up in bed, shirtless and disoriented. I had laid out my clothes the night before. I always do this when I know I am waking up early and will be mindlessly stumbling around like a zombie in the A.M.

I dress in silence, stumble down the stairs, make my way to the truck and then on to the job. It's a big job today meaning a big crew. The day starts out relatively smoothly.

The air is suddenly combustible, Mick had walked from the front of the truck around to the back and was yelling at all of us.

"Who drank my Vitamin water?" Mick is a theater kid. Working as a mover until he get his break on Broadway. He is very young, handsome and strong and some of the crew are jealous.

It's now 10 a.m. We have been working for several hours loading the truck. We all stop and look over at him. He continues, "Ok, which one of the c**** took a sip from my drink and put it back?"

I had not done it, but the idea of someone taking a drink from his beverage, putting the lid back on and then placing it back in his bag strikes me as hilarious. Taking it and stealing it is mean. But taking a sip and putting it back is trolling someone at expert level. Simmons, who is at the back of the truck, starts to laugh.

Mick turns his attention to Simmons. Mick's eyes widen and he looks at Simmons with murderous rage, "Did you take the drink from my bag?"

Simmons looks at the floor and smiles sheepishly. "Nah, man, I just think it's funny."

Mick doesn't say anything.

Simmons continues. "I mean it's funny that someone put it back," he says, trying not to laugh.

I can't hold it together anymore and start to laugh. I look at Mick apologetically. "It wasn't me man. I have been upstairs the whole time, you know that." It is true. I had been upstairs, I just came down for more blankets and it isn't me, but now I can't stop laughing and it makes me look very guilty.

We are working on a 5th floor walk-up. We normally break up the work by forming a makeshift "water brigade". After an initial peek at the apartment, I was assigned the 4th to the 2nd floor, one of the worst spots. Since I was just hired, it's normal for the new guy to get the stairs. I take items from the point (or foreman), who then walks them down one floor to me. I then walk them down two flights and then the guy below me walks them down one flight and then Mick takes them from him and walks them down one flight and then out to the truck. Then on the truck, Simmons takes the items and packs the truck.

The apartment is located in the village and while a beautiful locale, the building itself is cramped and dreary. Over 100 years old, it has those tiny stairs that are better suited to little hobbits' feet rather than my oafish, filthy, size 13 Adidas. The apartment is unique like a lot of these old buildings. It features a beautiful skylight that lets the light stream in, I can only imagine the joy it brings to the dreary Januarys that NYC offers. But the door frame in the kitchen is the opposite of glamour. It is low, very low, so low that I have to duck each time I enter and exit the little room.

Down come the items. Boxes, TVs, beds, and couches all filter down through the narrow hallways and stairwells, down, down, down, to the street and then on to the truck. To their new temporary home in the truck, stacked in their little cell until delivered, hopefully intact and unscathed, to their new residence. On the truck the person assigned there is a real-life player in a game of Tetris. Simmons, in this case, is assigned today and loads the items trying to maximize the space, placing the boxes on top of one another like Legos. That is, of course, unless he is busy breaking seals on new beverages and taking swigs from co-workers' drinks.

This load from this man's apartment is only the first part of the move. This job has a second part. The move is a combination of two people's households. We finish packing up the things at this man's hobbit like dwelling and then move on to the second location.

The second location is at 570 Fort Washington Ave in Washington Heights. It's as far north as you can be and still be in Manhattan. It is amazing that these two stayed together, this is a very long distance relationship by NYC standards. The street itself is relatively quiet, if a little hilly.

The building is pedestrian, but its entrance is striking. It is a clear example of Art Deco design with its horizontal orientation. The entrance is headlined by the very large digits 570 also in the Art Deco font. The hole in the zero is nearly half-filled in as is the hole in the bottom half of the 5. It's the same font used in the infamous Studio 54 disco that dominated the late 70s and early 80s, right in Midtown Manhattan.

The entrance almost seems modeled in the same style as the book Atlas Shrugged, that book that has caused so many disagreements between my brothers and me. We each have read the book and have seen what we want to see in it. The "Smith boys like to fight" is what my kids' mom used to say. I half expected the main character, John Galt, to come waltzing out the front door carrying a hat and a briefcase. The lobby is elegant. Clearly designed in the 80s. Marble floors and perfectly clean couches from the 70s. The whole thing looks like a museum— beautiful, clean, and slightly uncomfortable.

As we get up to the apartment, the couple is in the back having a whispered meeting about what to keep. This is a much larger apartment than the first one with too many things to fit on the truck. She has much more stuff than she confirmed on the inventory. There is a delightful, elegant, antique elevator lined with a rich dark wood which at some point was probably worked by an elevator man with a circular little hat with a strap. We begin to wheel the things down to the elevator, praying that the larger items will fit. We squeeze as much as we can into the truck and leave the rest behind in her apartment.

The day drags on but wraps up nicely, fortunately avoiding an accident with a double-parked taxi down a narrow street, that was a very close call. I park the truck and make the weary trip home to my apartment. The way the day went, we weren't able to break for lunch and by the time I get home I am hungry enough to piggishly eat anything, and I do.

I fall into a carb induced food coma while watching Netflix. The laptop on my stomach has heated up almost searing my skin. I am stirred from my slumber by a familiar voice. It takes me a second and then I realize, the lady is back. My Neflix is paused with the familiar "Are you still watching?" question. I put it off to the side. I slowly get to my feet and peer out the window to see a much better, or at least more realistic show, than what I was watching on the computer. These characters in the middle of my street are more layered than what couldn't hold my interest on the streaming service. Even with the limited information I have, this lady's story intrigues me.

As I look out the window, I can see that she is not alone. My now favorite human alarm clock is pulling a giant man. He is at least 6′5″ with a huge belly and a mostly bald head. As they get closer to my apartment, I can start to make out the words and I open my window quietly to improve my chances of hearing.

"Give me my spare key back and...," the man bellows before being interrupted.

"No, not right now. Don't worry, I'll get it back to you," she replies.

"I'm not playing around. I'm serious. It's over. I want my spare key."

"Don't do this now. It's late. I'm scared," she replies. She is now literally hanging on him. Holding on to him with all she has. This is the end. I can feel the desperation and sadness in her voice even from here, 100 feet away.

She repeats over and over how scared she is.

I look bleary-eyed at the clock on my phone, it's 3 a.m. I heard the beginning of this argument yesterday morning at 5 a.m. It has to have been a long day for these two. The back-and-forth continues and I ease away from the window sitting on the back of my couch, like a nosy old lady. I've been out of my regular routine lately and for some reason I'm very curious as to what is going on in the lives of others.

They keep walking, eventually stopping where one of the lights from the house across the street is lighting up the avenue. I can see the man clearly for the first time. He is a man's man. He isn't wearing a mask. His face is the face of a man who has worked hard all his life. Very blue collar. Perhaps early 50s. The large beer belly puffing out the front of his white T-shirt so much that you can see a little of the belly popping out the bottom. Hugging him, holding on tight is the woman. Her voice is cracking and desperate as she pleads with him. She keeps repeating,

"I'm scared. I'm scared."

As she hugs him, his arms stay loose at his sides, but she tries to wrap herself around him like a wayward vine. He from time to time tries to extricate himself from her grasp, but she adjusts her grip and denies his attempts to wiggle away.

This back-and-forth persists: her crying and trying to hold him, and him wanting to leave. In the end he relents.

"Ok, I'll get the key tomorrow. You have to go inside now."

"Ok, you said, you promised," she says and slowly releases him. Being released, he immediately retreats like a freed bird. She takes a step onto the stoop and he quickly walks off down the street shaking his head furiously and mumbling to himself.

"Call me tomorrow," she yells after him.

"Uh huh," he replies but his intention unclear, he is focusing on his escape.

The woman slowly moves up the steps watching him power walk off into the night. Then she gets to her door, fumbles with the key, eventually opening the door, entering, closing the door and exiting this very public scene. I never see either of them on the street again.

I retreat to the warmth of my bed and close the window. We all need love and affection. Most of us are scared of being alone or dying alone. But you can't make somebody love you. You can't make somebody feel something they don't feel. They will not love you just because you love them. They will not forgive you just because you forgive them. I'm not sure what this lady did to this man, if anything, and I'll never know. But she apologized to him at least 50 times that I witnessed. She can't make him forgive her.

Today at the end of the workday, Mick approached the whole crew sheepishly. "I think I drank my own drink now that I think of it. Sorry about that guys." And in that moment, we had to forgive him.

In the end, everyone chooses their own path. And long-term, regardless of how hard you try, or how much you want it, you cannot force someone to love you or to forgive you. It must be freely given. It is said love is the purest gift you can give others. Give it to yourself once in a while too, you deserve it.

Romulus

It's my turn to drive. I'm bouncing down the freeway driving a 28-foot moving truck that is tagged with suggestive graffiti and competing gang signs. Burrito in one hand, Taco Bell Mild Sauce in the other. I'm living, man. It's like the movie Speed except, less Keanu Reeves and more acid reflux and closet fat guy. You know, in shape until I take my shirt off and you go, "Ohhhh, now I see where all those Little Debbie Swiss cupcakes go."

Today I'm driving with Justin. Justin has connected his phone to the radio and is playing his high school buddies' band. "Aren't they great?" he yells over the country music. No, they aren't. I can unequivocally say it's disturbingly hard to listen to. The instruments sound ok, but the singer sounds like a cat being strangled, slowly. But I keep these thoughts to myself.

"Uh huh," I say in response, taking another bite of burrito and using the excuse of having my mouth full to not discuss the recording of this poor animal's abuse. I'm dripping burrito sauce on the steering wheel and my shorts. This is a very high-end operation, clearly.

We are on our way to the Finger Lakes. A young couple, after dating a few months during the pandemic, has decided to escape Brooklyn and buy a house in Romulus. You know, Romulus named after Romulus, the son of Mars the god of war from Roman mythology. A warning shot if there ever was one.

I took this move knowing full well that I have to be back in the city for a show tonight, my spot is at 11 p.m. We can make it if we hurry and Justin doesn't do his usual lallygagging.

Earlier in the day we had stopped by a storage locker. Apparently, this couple put all their stuff in one locker back in March at the beginning of the pandemic shutdown and ran out of Dodge. The same moving company that I am with had moved them into the locker and I'm sorry to say they had done an abominable job. There was a table that was not just cracked, but fully broken, and a couch that had not been properly covered up and was now dirty, specifically where a bike had been placed on top of it.

The problem with running a moving company is that it is hard to find good people. The job is very physical, which rules out much interest from most of the population. But, if you really want to get in shape and get your step count up while carrying weighted objects, do I have a job for you. In NYC it is not uncommon to have to move people out of 5th floor walk-ups. A 5th floor walk-up is exactly that: you have to walk up. There is no elevator or escalator or flying balloon. You have to walk. Additionally, the staircase may have been built 100 years ago, when apparently grown men wore size 6 shoes. The steps are often very narrow, requiring me to turn my feet sideways when descending while carrying an oversized La-Z-Boy, all the time under the watchful eye of a client. Lazy boy, indeed.

The starting pay is $20 per hour, which is very close to the $15 per hour city minimum. Additionally, this job does not have any sick days, vacation days, holidays, 401k, or even coffee breaks. There is often not even a place to relieve yourself, so you are left to your own devices, but that is a story for a different time. By now, you are probably asking yourself why I would take this job? Excellent question. If you have any other options, then by all means, take them. Even at McDonalds you'll work in air conditioning, have steady hours, and free Big Macs. Here you do not, and as a consequence, workers come and go. Sometimes they go away for a long while, which is code for prison. Sometimes they go away for a short while, which is code for jail.

So, who wrapped this filthy couch and where are they now? Who knows, possibilities are wide and varied; he could be in Rikers Island, Sing Sing, Attica, or any other world famous lockup. Or maybe he got another job, any job, and thought this was for the birds. In any case, he is not here now. He has taken his cash from the job and moved on, not thinking once about the storage locker and its dismal contents. What it comes down to is, we're here now and we're going to have to remedy it.

We start the load at 9 a.m. Before that, I had taken a train to Brooklyn to pick up a rental truck from a place that stays open 24 hours. It is a corner lot in a poorly lit part of town. There were already three people in line before me when I got there at 7:45. Most people come to NYC to make their dreams happen. They come to work. There is no space in your apartment to hang out. You have no living room. The city is your living room. Most people come to grind out a living and then leave. Sometimes they have an exit plan when they arrive. An old classmate of mine said to me, "I can stand three more years. I already found a place in Massachusetts in the country. When I turn 40, I'm out!" That level of excitement for moving to a dilapidated farm in the middle of nowhere is something only NYC can induce.

When we unlock the doors, we find the storage unit is filled to the brim with clutter. Some people might call it stuff, but I feel a connection with you and should be honest. It's mostly garbage. You can say it in the French way if you want, garBAJ, the way people do with Target, but it doesn't change the fact. This is a mishmash of items that would be more at home at the dump. There is a 5 foot-long, 6 inch in circumference column that is painted gold for some reason and the base of an old Singer sewing machine that is held together with plastic ties. There are forty crumbling boxes that have wilted in the soggy east coast weather and a painter's bucket full of tools with seven rolls of quarters. The quarters are a vestige of living in Manhattan too long where you need them for laundry. The couple's new house in the burbs will for sure have a washing machine that does not need quarters, but some habits die hard.

It's over 90 degrees by the time we finish loading the truck at 11 a.m., we are doing great on time. The box truck is made of fiberglass and metal and heats up like a walk-in sauna. Today it is my turn to move things around the inside of the truck, cramming the furniture inside like ill-shaped sardines so we can fit in everything from the storage unit. The inside of the truck is well over 110 degrees Fahrenheit. There is a certain order that the truck is normally loaded to maximize space. Boxes first. But today we had to take the items out of the storage unit before we were ready to load them.

The items were "staged," which is what it's called when we set the items off to the side to allow for boxes to go in first.

The load goes relatively smoothly considering much of it is not boxed or wrapped. Today I am teamed up with Lanza and Justin. Lanza is still sporting that 18-inch beard and looking like he's ready to tour with Linkin Park.. He is wearing black shorts, black shirt, black hat, and white socks.

Lanza tells me, "Before this I was a camera man and a grip." The word 'this' is a stand in for the pandemic. Many people are displaced and looking for something to do. Few people dream of becoming a mover. I have never heard a child say, "Maybe someday when I grow up, I can go into a disheveled man's apartment and help him carry out boxes that hold the remnants of his broken NYC dreams."

"Did you work on anything I would know?" I ask, trying not to drop my end of a music cabinet made in the 70s that weighs several hundred pounds. Have these people never heard of MP3 players?

Lanza looks like he is going to pass out. "Mostly I worked on Impractical Jokers. Have you heard of it?" Everyone has heard of it. It's a cleaner version of the TV show Jackass, clean enough for the whole family to watch it. Probably one of the few shows a family could agree on when three generations get together.

"Yeah, I'm using this money to just survive. I don't know if I'm too old to be doing this job. I mean I'm 31 now, I don't know if my body can take it." He puts down his end of the music cabinet to finish telling me the story, while I continue to hold my end.

I smile and tell him, "I think you'll be alright" and point with my lips to the cabinet that I am still holding up, only now completely alone. I 'm 46. I would hit this man in the face with this stupid gold painted wooden column to be 31 again. I'm a full 50% older than him. But I smile and he, thankfully, picks his end back up.

"I'm saving this money. I'm going to use it for a down payment for a house up in Syracuse. I mean, why stay here, there is no work, and I can't even sit in La Colombe," Lanzo says. He has a point; La Colombe has excellent coffee. It is, however, a chain and can be found outside NYC. But I will not be the one to tell him. As we maneuver the music cabinet out of the unit and onto the truck, I've decided Lanzo is for sure leaving NYC. It might be August; it might be September, but he's leaving. Four hundred and fifty thousand people left NYC in the first 30 days of the pandemic. Are they coming back? Who knows, but not this month. This month almost all of our moves are outbound. There are a few moves within the city. People whose leases are up, and they are looking to move into better places with lower prices. Sharing an apartment during a pandemic is not ideal for most people.

Lanzo is only working on the load of the storage unit. The actual drive-up to the house and unload falls on Justin and me. Justin is 39. He has a beard of fashionable length, but you can still see his dimples. His hair falls at his shoulders and he hides most of it under a hat.

"I came to the city to model mostly," he says.

I raise my eyebrows and weakly smile. "Oh, cool." It's possible, he's tallish and good looking.

"But the lady who got me to come was mostly running a scam. I ended up sleeping on the floor. Man, so weird." I turn my head back to listen. Now I'm interested.

"But I did do some modeling, mostly runway and print. Oh, and voiceover stuff. Oh, and I can do auctioneer stuff." Justin launches into an auctioneer rant trying to drive up the price; now I can hear clearly the Virginia twang in his voice.

"25 do I hear a 30, 35 to a 40?" He keeps going. The pacing is good, it's intelligible and very fast. As far as I know I am not casting for anything right now, let alone an auctioneer, but he has my vote.

"That was great, you have my vote," I tell him. He's beaming and smiles warmly, his dimples showing through the beard.

"Yeah, so after that I did some teaching at the high school and worked at a fancy gym with fancy people. Man, there are some girls there. Wow!" he whistled. He also shook his head slowly from side to side. Again showing me that those girl were attractive, in case I didn't understand his words and whistle.

"But the thing is man, they want it all. They want the money, and the job and the looks and all of it. Not many guys have all of it. And if they do, they can be with supermodels." Justin shakes his head as he tries to dispel that notion with the violence of his head movements. "When they meet me, they say, 'Oh baby you're fit. Are you an athlete?' and I tell 'em, 'Nah, I'm a mover. They hate that.'" He laughs at the thought.

It's a five hour drive each way to this little city named after one of the founders of Rome. Legend has it that Rome was founded by twin brothers Romulus and Remus who suckled at a she-wolf. It's a long story. Rome was named after Romulus. Remus was killed by his brother and banished to the annals of history. The only other Remus I have ever heard of is Uncle Remus, and he wasn't even real.

Romulus, N.Y. is nothing like Rome, but they do have an Olive Garden, so there is that. They also have wineries and a brewery that Justin talked about for a good hour on the ride up.

"No man, I came up here last summer. I met some girl in the city, and she had a cabin up here on Seneca Lake. Crazy weekend man. There are these two Thai sisters. One of them, Penny, only dates athletes and Meg only dates old rich guys. They like successful guys. They have been taken to the Super Bowl like six times by different dates. Penny and Meg run this little restaurant in Brooklyn, but they also bartend on the side; they both have like four jobs. So, we get up to the cabin, next stop the brewery…" I zone out. This road feels like it is bouncing my organs directly on to the seats with each pothole we hit. There are farms on the sides of the road. Massive cows lie lazily in fields. Billboards rise and fall peddling everything from fast food to new homes. I see two deer on the side of the road unaware on how close they are to death if they take only a few more steps onto the freeway.

"We have to go back to that place man. You know?"

There is a pause; oh right, it's a conversation not a monologue. I answer. "Yeah bud, I just want to not crash the truck and unload all this stuff."

"You'll be fine. I crashed a truck last week."

"You did?"

"Yeah, there are bolts on the Manhattan Bridge. Did you know that? I didn't know that, yeah, I didn't see them. I had to pay for the repair to the truck, 1500 bucks. If you crash it, you have to pay. Did you know that?"

I didn't know, but now I do. When I started here last month, I was asked if I drive. I said yes, remember no one even asked to see my license. This is a very trusting group of disorganized movers. "You look like you have a pulse. Want to drive a sixty thousand dollar truck up to the Canadian border?" Sure, what could possibly go wrong? Well, apparently you could hit something on the Manhattan Bridge.

He asks where I'm living, and I tell him I'm moving to Brooklyn. "Where are you living?" I ask expecting a pedestrian answer of one of the boroughs or perhaps New Jersey.

"I don't really have a place right now. I mean, I have money, I have those rental properties in Virginia, so I'm doing fine."

He can see the concern on my face. "Don't worry, I'm not homeless." He pauses. "I'm just between homes, since 2016," he clarifies.

He is in a great mood considering he has been without permanent shelter for four years. Someone should tell him he's homeless. But that's above my pay grade.

"I have money saved. There are a lot of people who aren't prepared for this financial crisis. I am man. I have money saved. I used to run a pizza shop and the building was run down. The owner didn't care and there was always something wrong with that building. I am so happy to be out of that. Now all I do is show up and move that from here to there. It's so great man. I love it." His face breaks into a big, relaxed smile. He lifts his hat off his head and runs his fingers through his now visible clearly thinning hair. It is mostly brown, but there is a mix of grey and white. He could have modeled. He has an easy confidence and dark blue eyes.

"I gave up my place in December of 2016 and never looked back. Sometimes I stay with my buddy in Jackson Heights, sometimes with my other buddy in the village, sometimes at my baby mama's house. The key is always to have clothes with you." He points to a duffel bag that is on the bench between us.

We are almost there when we pass through the town of Ovid, N.Y. Someone cleverly has added the letter C to the sign so that it reads C Ovid. It looks as if the letter C was added, covered up and then added again.

"Oh, man, I need to get a picture of that." Justin has taken over driving and pulls over. I don't mind the way he drives; the problem is that when he drives, he will use any excuse to stop and turn an 8-hour job into a 17-hour ordeal. He doesn't ask; he just starts driving to the new destination or adds a stop. Short jobs in the city we are paid by the hour, but for long moves it is by the job. We don't get paid until it's done. We are not done until he stops making extra stops and we can return the truck. One is left sounding like an angry stepmom asking, where are we going now? "It's cool man, it will be fun." Will it? Thanks for deciding for me. That's what all grown men like in life is to have someone else make their decisions for them assuring them a longer work day.

After a couple of unscheduled stops, we finally arrive at the house. It is on Lake Seneca, just like he said. We meet Rachel for the first time. She hired us for the move. They are remodeling an older home and there is a dumpster out front full of what was, until recently, the interior of this house.

"You guys made it, great. Let me get some water." She says. We are already sweating before we begin the unload. There is no AC in the truck and that front window cooks up the cab like a greenhouse.

"Man, that lake is great, I want to jump in it," Justin replies.

"Sure, if you want," Rachel says a little unsure on how to take these two scruffy, sweaty guys (one who has spilled taco sauce on his shorts) now in her driveway.

"Ok, where do you want to put the stuff?" Justin says still looking out at the lake.

"I want most of the stuff in the back room except the stuff that goes in the room off of the garage." I bite my tongue and don't ask, "You sure you don't want us to just throw all this in the dumpster? I feel like it matches it perfectly." Instead, we start to unload the things from the truck. She wants to decide where each item is to go as it's coming off the truck, but she is having a hard time deciding and reverses herself several times. When you're carrying heavy items, seconds feel like minutes and minutes feel frustrating. To make matters worse I unload the table that is broken.

Justin starts talking about it.

"We took pictures when we picked it up, but it was already damaged. You can reach out to the office to ask for them to cover fixing the table. Also, if you clean that couch you can send the office the bill; they should cover it."

She is very upset. She is maybe 5'1" and a woman of average size. Dark hair and maybe Italian or Greek features. She is dressed in athletic gear as if we interrupted her work out.

Justin asks her, "Normally when we move stuff like this, we recommend that you wrap the items. Did they not tell you to wrap the items?"

Rachel, "Yeah they did, it's just that it is so expensive."

Yeah, well there you go. If you don't wrap the stuff it's going to get broken, no matter how rubbishy the stuff is. She calls her boyfriend. He comes around back. He is 6'2". Athletic build very curly blondish hair. He is low-key with kind eyes. "Hey, the movers." He raises his hands triumphantly over his head. "Real men doing real work," he says almost apologetically. He is accompanied by several of his friends. He tells us they're doing a version of the Highland Games in the back yard in front of the lake. Ben is his name.

I am holding an oversized box that like me is slowly falling apart. I am sweating and waiting for direction on where it goes.

"That's ok, let's just put all of it over here and we will sort it out," he says to Rachel and us.

No problemo man. Want it all outside is fine with me. Rachel and he have a low volume discussion about where to put things. She is not happy. He is hunched over, hands open, trying to please her; it is going so, so. It's a verbal tango that I have seen and participated in many times. Justin and I carry in several loads as the discussion continues. Being deaf in my right ear thanks to Covid is sometimes an unmitigated blessing, as in this case, where I cannot hear the conversation at all. The discussion ends.

Ben has his friends help carry a few things from the garage into the house to where Rachel wants them. I offer that we can help carry the stuff inside, but he wants to do it with his friends.

Apparently, there is still a lot to do in the house and they disagree on when to move things in, now or later.

This move includes a lot of driftwood and pieces of wood eaten by termites that have produced unusual patterns. It is going to be turned into art I'm told. I believe you man. Just tell me where you want me to put it.

We finally finish unloading everything. Justin talks to Rachel and Ben about the three items that are damaged. It's hard to tell what they will do. Justin tells her she can email the office. Ben says, "Meh, it's fine." Not sure what action they will take. Rachel pays him the remainder of the job in cash and a tip. He doesn't count it and puts it in his pocket.

Before we leave, we have to fold up the moving blankets and then put the dollies back on the truck. If we leave now, we can get back to the city, I can shower and take a quick nap, that's great.

"Want to split up the cash?" I ask. That's the only reason I do this job. Normally, that is what we do--split the cash when it's paid. We also normally count it to make sure we are not short.

"We will when we get on the road," he says.

Justin heads back to the cab of the truck with, "I'm going to jump in the lake." He had mentioned that on the drive up, but I thought that was an expression I have a vague recollection of hearing in my childhood. 'Go jump in a lake' is something my grandpa might have said. Apparently, he meant it.

He emerges from the cab with a towel that he had thoughtfully brought with him. It is now 5 p.m. I have been working nine hours and we still have a 5-hour drive back to turn in the truck and then get home. I'm not amused, but he has the keys and is not asking my permission. I'm the new guy and I am reminded of that every day. How can you be the new guy when you're almost an antique? I begrudgingly wander down to the dock. Sure enough, Justin almost has his swimsuit on.

The lake is beautiful. There are very few people out there. There are a couple of fishing boats 200 yards north but no one closer on the water. Ben and Rachel are inside discussing where things go, but I guess we are done. The light is reflecting off the lake hitting the structure on the dock that is used to raise and lower boats on the water.

Justin is already in the water and swimming.

"How is it?" I ask.

"Oh man, it's great," he says, "Almost too hot." In no time he is 80 yards out. We are not going anywhere any time soon. I look out to the water; it is beautiful here. I look back to the house. No one around. What's the difference? I strip down to my underwear which is black and could pass for a swimsuit at 100 feet distance. I dive in. The water is cold.

"You liar," I yell out to Justin. "There is no way this is hot," I laugh. It's refreshing considering I have been sweating for eight hours straight, but it is definitely not hot. I swim out a little and feel the seaweed on my legs. It is quiet up here. I can hear the water lapping on my face and Justin splashing, but not much else.

An older man dressed in cargo shorts and a red t-shirt is walking by the dock. Maybe he'll keep walking. Nope, he walks right out to the dock and out onto it. He is being led by an older Jack Terrier. He is mostly bald and has a cigarette held loosely on his lips, the ash needs to be shaken from the end but stubbornly refuses to fall.

"Nice out there huh?" he yells out.

"Yeah, it's great." Justin yells back. "You have a house out here"?

"No, my son just bought this house." He points back at the house full of the junk we just unloaded.

They start talking about the weather and the power plant at one end of the lake. I swim a little more hoping he'll bounce out of here so I can exit in my underwear. No dice. They are now talking about the mayor of NYC. The man talks about how he misses Bloomberg and all I can think is "I'm glad there is not a stop-and-frisk on this dock when I get out in my underwear."

I swim for about 30 minutes eavesdropping on a conversation that devolves into politics, my second least favorite subject to listen to when I'm stripped down to my underwear. Eventually I have stalled enough and decide to get out of the water. These two could start their own podcast and call it Lakeside Poli Talk for all I care. I'm getting out of the lake.

I climb the metal ladder onto the dock. There is no beach here; it's all stone and zebra mussels that will slice your feet up quicker than an old man with a Jack Terrier can talk to you about politics. I climb out a few feet from where the man in cargo shorts is standing giving Justin a speech about the budget deficit. I pretend to not be in my underwear and he pretends not to notice. We're almost like an old, married couple each ignoring the other and seeing only what they choose to see and little else.

I do that old surfer's trick where you wrap the towel around your waist and remove your underwear and put your shorts on, all the while showing the world nothing.
"Hey bud, we should be heading back," I say after I'm safely covered up.

"Oh yeah," Justin says like we are on a leisurely family vacation and not about to restart a journey that will end at midnight at this pace.

Eventually, he gets out and we say our goodbyes to the old man and his dog who is afraid of the water. I offer to drive, hoping to avoid a series of stops that may include the world's largest ball of string.

"No, I got it," he says. I consider my options. Should I wrestle the keys from him? Maybe I should have gone through his pockets when he was in the water and freed those keys from this dilly-dallier. We climb into the cab. It's 5:30 p.m. Ok, if we leave now, I can still make it, no nap but I can still shower and perform.

Exiting the driveway Justin turns to the left. We should be turning to the right. "I think we need to go right. South is that way." I say pointing south.

"Yeah, I know but there is a brewery up here I want to check out." I almost slap myself on the forehead. I should have gone through his pockets when he was in the water. That was my golden opportunity.

He can see the look on my face. "Don't worry, it's close. We'll have one beer and we'll be out."

I am worried that I will never see my loved ones again. This guy stretches out shortcuts. After heading north for 20 minutes we pass it, then we come back around. I have looked it up on Google Maps. "Sorry man, it closed at 6 p.m." I tell him, faking my best disappointed face. "It's a pandemic you know. I guess we should go back."

"Man, that's a shame, ok, well let's at least go up the driveway and peak in." I want to strangle him.

We drive up the driveway and circle around. It's closed and we head down the road.
If we go straight back to the city now, I can't nap or shower, but I'm pretty clean from the lake, I could just go perform in the city as is. It would be tight, but I could barely make it.

We get about 20 minutes down the road and he pulls over. It is a fruit stand and I guess we are stopping. This is the third stop so far on the way home. I said I would drop him off in Jersey so he could see his kids and would take the truck back myself. Adding another hour to my day. He takes $20 out of the money we were just paid and jumps out.

"Want anything?" he asks.

"I'll jump out and see what they got." I don't want anything, but I certainly don't want to sit in a truck without AC on a hot day while he tells the Amish how they're missing out by not listening to his buddies' band.

The fruit stand is run by an Amish man with his half dozen blond, blue-eyed kids staring at the colorful but suggestive designs on the truck like we just landed from Mars. How do these people make enough money to survive?

I decide to buy some stuff. I buy a pie, two packages of cookies, some cinnamon rolls, tomatoes, cucumbers, and pickles. Then I see some spicy dill string beans.

"These are spicy?" I ask, not sure what I expect in reply. "Oh yeah, let me look at those," the Amish farmer says grabbing them with his thick fingers. Those are working man's hands, thick joints and dirt under the nails.

"They are spicy alright. Let me check the ingredients. Yep, there it is. I think it's the garlic. That makes them spicy." Ok, well spicy is a matter of perspective, but I'm sold.

There were four more stops and three terrible album repeats, I did not make the show.

I arrive home in Brooklyn at 2:15 a.m. Brooklyn isn't Rome, but I'm starting to understand why legend has it that Romulus killed his twin brother Remus. Did Remus also take too many rest stops? Perhaps he played ancient uninspired rock music that irritated Romulus until one day he snapped. Or perhaps he snapped cause he was constantly trying to test if all roads lead to Rome. Either way, they say Rome wasn't built in a day. And if it was built with the urgency that Justin shows, I can understand the hold up.

Down Under

Today I am working with William. William is from Australia. Perth to be exact.

"I'm from Perth. Well, Fremantle to be exact," he tells me.

"Oh cool, I loved Fremantle. I did a gig down at the Comedy Factory downtown Fremantle, you ever been?" I reply.

"Nah, I left Australia 15 years ago. I haven't been back since."

"Oh wow, what have you been up to in the States?"

"A little of this and a little of that. Bartending mostly, I guess." He pauses and puts down what he is carrying.

"I mostly wasted my life," he said somberly.

I was not ready for that kind of honesty this early in the morning and waited to see if there was a punch line or something else to defuse the tension, but there wasn't. He picked the coffee table back up and placed it on the truck with a thud.

Well, that's a bummer, I try to cheer him up, "Nah, don't think like that man," I said meagerly, but I could hear the sound of defeat in my own voice. I felt bad for him. He turned and walked back into the building to retrieve more belongings that we could not afford. This client's things are very nice and extremely expensive. We are moving them out of the financial district, an apartment located a block from the South Seaport, which is on the lower east side, between the Brooklyn Bridge and the Hugh Carey Tunnel. Facing the water, you can see Brooklyn Bridge on the left and all the NY Waterway Ferries moving people around the city. In the summer there is lawn furniture set up on the pier for people to soak up the weather. We are moving him to the village.

This move had started off on a weird foot from the very beginning. The move had been on the schedule for a while and the process is for the point to text the client to confirm the job. He then texts the other guys on the job and confirms the start time and details. Normally the text comes in around 5:00 p.m. the night before. However, in this case, 7:00 p.m. comes and goes with no text. Eleven p.m., no text. At midnight, I call the point.

"Yo Todd, we have a move tomorrow at 7:00 a.m.?"

He sounds confused, "Who is this?"

Who do you think it is? Someone you work with at the moving company, sweet cheeks, is what I think, but what I say is: "This is Kirk. Do we have a move tomorrow at 7:00 a.m. on the lower east side?"

"No," he quickly answers and then adds, "I don't think so." Then there is another pause. "Let me call you back."

I get a call back 5 minutes later, "Yo, we have a move tomorrow at 7:00 a.m.," he says to me with no acknowledgement that I was the one who just told him that on the last call.

"Oh? You don't say." I can't help but let slip out.

"Yeah, I'll text you the address. Can you please be on time? See you tomorrow bud."

Can I please be on time? I'm the only reason he's going to show up at the job at all...is what I think, but what I say is, "You got it, see you tomorrow." You have to choose your battles.

As mentioned, the apartment we are emptying is lavishly decorated. If I had to choose one item to represent this client's things, it would be the lamp. It is one of those long drooping lamps, over 10 feet long and nearly impossible to pack or fit in an elevator. Also, it is very fragile and heavy, every mover's least favorite combination. There are over 20 boxes that are all marked fragile and heavy, normally heavy goes on bottom of the stack and fragile goes on the top. How do you suppose we pack these? Your guess is as good as mine.

The shiny expensive things come down one by one. Todd is up in the apartment wrapping. William and I are taking the items down the elevator and another 100 feet to the end of the block where the truck is parked. It is parked illegally in front of a fire hydrant, but not blocking the road.

I had asked William if he had a girlfriend and he is now walking me through all the relationships he has had since arriving in the States.

He continues, "Yeah, I loved that girl, but we just couldn't make it work. I tried. I gave it my best. But I think when someone is done, they are done. Don't drop this, it's marble." He added the last bit as he handed me a small, circular but very heavy end table.

He continued to describe his last relationship that ended poorly.

"Yeah, she ripped my heart out, but I really loved the b****." He tells me staring soberly at the end table and not seeing the irony of the comment. I carry the end table deeper into the truck. There is a moment of silence.

I look up to see Todd bounding down the street. "This is it." he yells slightly lifting his arms to highlight the things he is carrying.

"We out," he adds for emphasis. William walks down to Todd to grab something out of his arms.

We arrive at the new apartment, which is much more spacious, but less luxurious. We begin to unload the things.

This is my last move of the summer. My last move with the company. I am not one of their main guys and when the winter comes, I will not be needed. I saved enough to buy JJ his car so I'm at peace about it.

Two weeks later I fly to Sweden to see JJ. Yes, I am going to see my son and buy him his car the long-awaited purchase of the summer. The flight is long with multiple connections and then the several hundred mile drive up from the airport to his place. I have checked two bags. I travel light. Half a dozen shirts and underwear for me, but I'm weighed down with gifts for him.

When a child has only one parent in Latin America he is referred to as an orphan, meaning he is missing a parent. I think that idea is appropriate here too. With one of the parents gone, there is something missing. The package of two parents is broken and it's less than ideal; he knows it, if only subconsciously. Like many parents, I try to overcompensate by buying gifts. The thought that another cool t-shirt from Uniqlo is going to replace his mother is fantasy, yet here I am again with 100 pounds of "stuff" that I hope will fill what is missing from his heart. Some habits die hard.

The first day I see him I greet him warmly, but tentatively. Unsure of how he'll react. I have a daily video call with him, but I still have a deep, unfounded fear he will forget me. These fears are short lived. As soon as I open the door, he is excited to see me and wants to be tickled. It is carried over from when he was 200 pounds lighter but one that brings memories of a simpler time. Nearly 20 years later, I am still happy to oblige. We are both happy and have a great day, including a trip to his favorite fast-food place appropriately called Big Boy.

The next day I start the car shopping process. All summer as I slowly saved money from each move, I had been looking online for appropriate vehicles. Now, I am excited to finish the process. This represents a new chapter in his life. While he will not be driving himself, the idea of him having his own car and the independence surrounding it excites me. Another big step for my big boy.

After narrowing it down to a few options I opt for a small compact car that will be inexpensive to maintain and hopefully reliable. After handing over the cash to the dealer, I am excited to take him on a drive in it. One our first drives together he jumps in like he understands my explanation of this being his car. We drive through the woods and make our way around the coastline of the Baltic Sea that lines the east coast of Sweden.

As the car winds through the picturesque scenery, JJ sits in the front seat silently with headphones on playing Abba on his phone loud enough that I can hear it. He stares out the window quietly, listening to opening bars of Dancing Queen blasting though his headphones. What is he thinking? I have no idea. He is mostly nonverbal and he keeps his innermost thoughts to himself. It is a quiet and serene three-hour drive. We stop for gas and snacks and then make our way back to his home. I park in front of his house. He gets out of the car, comes to the driver's side, and lightly touches his forehead to mine. He has done this since he was three. When he wants to connect with me, he touches forehead to forehead like the Maori in New Zealand.

I spend a great 10 days there in Sweden with him and then it is time to go.

There will be no more moves when I get back. The season is over and another chapter in my life is closed. This is not the first time a chapter of my life has unexpectedly and quickly opened, and just as quickly closed.

When I was young, I took a corporate job. My wife and I had just returned from working at an orphanage in Romania. We had come back pregnant and I needed to find a job with benefits. It was not my dream job, but I was starting a family and everyone in my house liked to eat. I toiled at it for some years. Days were busy at the office, nights and weekends were taken up with night school. In a few years I completed the MBA that I hoped would bring with whatever it was that I was unknowingly searching for. It did not. I then pursued working at a nonprofit for a few years, which I enjoyed immensely. It filled a part of me, but I still felt something was missing.

It was not until my 30s that I gained courage to chase what I really wanted: comedy. I had always liked making people laugh, but it was not until a full decade of searching that I found it. Taking a big pay cut to start a new career is nerve wracking, as was walking away from the stability of a normal job, but I knew that performing comedy brought me real joy I could not get from a regular 9 to 5 job. I finally found the missing piece I had been searching for in my corporate career. Those first few years of performing comedy were unpredictable and difficult, trying to find places that would let me perform for five minutes at a time, at 2:00 in the morning, for a bartender and waitress waiting to lock up for the night. However, with time I found my footing and more importantly, felt fulfilled in bringing joy to others through my words and jokes.

Similarly to my early years in comedy, this year has proven to be unpredictable and difficult, uncertain of what awaits me in the future. Instead of performing for comedy fans, I have now found myself lifting armoires and hutches. And I enjoyed it, not necessarily the lifting, but the process of helping people move to their new places to start over and chase their dreams.

Months later, just as abruptly as the job started, it has now ended. What will I do next? I'm not sure, but there is always another adventure around the corner. To prepare for the next adventure, we must release the bitterness and baggage we are carrying— it will not serve us. We all carry too much garbage, both literal and emotional. If I have learned one thing looking into people's apartments and lives, it's that they hold on to things too long. It's hard to receive something new and great when your hands and heart are full of so much clutter.

If the army refers to itself as a band of brothers, then this moving company could be described as a band of stepbrothers. In addition to learning how to wrap furniture with plastic wrap and to efficiently load a moving truck like a real-life game of Tetris, I have also learned some valuable life lessons from these dysfunctional stepbrothers.

First, you can't make someone do something they don't want to do. You can't make someone wake up at 5:00 a.m. to be at work on time. You can't make someone stay and finish the job carrying down furniture when they don't want to. You can't make someone keep their shoes on and not rub their feet if they really want to. That drive has to come from within. Surround yourself with people who have their own high motor and will encourage and push you on your days when you need that loving push. People are very different. Some people are into mornings, some evenings. Some into smoking, some nonsmokers. Some into colas and some into coffees (vigorously shaken early in the morning). Some into video games and some into movies. It doesn't matter. We are all different, but in many ways we are all the same, looking for love, compassion and kindness. The changes we think they should make have to come from within themselves, we cannot make them do something they don't want to do.

Second, life is infinitely unpredictable. Just when you think you have something steady, it changes, and then changes again. Your resiliency will serve you well. You are your own best and most unique product. You will find a way. Have a dream and pursue it. Don't give up. Every day is not a red-letter day. Life is filled with ordinary days and the only true measure of success is your resiliency. Even if you have to pay your workers in cash. Even if you have to budget thousands of dollars a year in parking tickets. Even if you measure success by counting how many fist fights you didn't get into at work. Keep working forward. To quote Winnie, that old British bulldog, "Never. Never. Never. Never give up."

When kings die there is an odd expression, "The king is dead. Long live the king." This king is gone, but there is a new king in his place. Life will continue to go on. The kingdom and its struggles continue. In life, each ending is a new opportunity for a beautiful beginning. The bitter mixed in with the sweet. Take in and mourn the bitter, but embrace and hold on to the sweet, which is right around the corner.

Third, it's never over until it's over. If you're reading this, you are alive and you can still do it. You may feel defeated, lost, or ready to surrender but it's never over until it's fully over. Your best work hasn't yet been completed, and perhaps not even started. Academy Award Winner Anthony Hopkins did not receive any recognition within the industry until he was 54. Years later, he has starred in countless award nominated movies in leading roles. Imagine if he had given up on his acting dream when he turned 50, or never started acting at all because of the fear of the unknown.

Some of us start later in life and that's perfectly fine. Your next adventure may be right around the corner waiting for you.

Back to the move. We pull into the new apartment where we have to unload the client's furniture for her next adventure. What will she do within the walls of this new building? Will she write a book, design a building, start a business, or have children? We will likely never know the answer to that question, but it's comforting to know that with this new adventure, the future is wide open.

"I'm moving back to Australia," William says suddenly over the truck's loud clamoring. We are done unpacking and are driving the empty truck back to some forgotten side street deep in Brooklyn. It had been a quiet ride punctuated now by William's proclamation.

"I'm going to do something else," he continued.

"Yeah, what are you going to do?" I ask.

"I have no idea, but it's going to be good. It's time to go home, I'll figure something out," he says taking out a pack of tobacco and some rolling papers.

"You're young, man, do it, you could change your name to Bill if you want," I say trying to sound encouraging.

"I'm not young," he replies. "But it doesn't matter, I need to do it. It's time."

He's right. It is time. It is always time.

Godspeed to Billy in Australia, JJ with his new car, and to you, whatever your next adventure may be. Please, just don't pack your treasure in black plastic garbage bags. You'll thank me later.

Acknowledgements

I could not have done this without my family's support. Specifically my mom's efforts. I have a bad habit of starting a sentence midway through a thought. She helped turn these half thoughts into fully formed expressions. To my brother Henry who helped with naming some of the chapters after our favorite song titles and pointing me towards to Our north star. To Zona Baker and Sarah Hall. Your editing, thoughts and effort lovingly poured into this little book transformed it. You have my eternal thanks. To Orlin for the art work and to countless others for your encouragement and love. And I would like to thank the protagonists of this book for being yourself. Without your colorful existence, there is not story. xo

Printed in Great Britain
by Amazon

64118842R00088